With Our Compliments

𝕸embership Department
American Management Associations

The Decentralized Company

The
Decentralized
Company

Making the Most of
Entrepreneurial Management

ROBERT E. LEVINSON

American Management Associations

Library of Congress Cataloging in Publication Data

Levinson, Robert E., 1925–
  The decentralized company.

  Includes index.
  1. Decentralization in management. I. Title.
HD50.L48 1983   658.4'02   82-16470
ISBN 0-8144-5674-X

First Printing

To my wife, Phyllis,
whose partnership in our marriage and business
has contributed to our mutual love and success.

Preface

This book puts forth an admittedly radical idea. It suggests that we reverse the trend toward management centralization that has been popular for lo these many years. It puts forth the case, not just for returning to decentralization in management, but for *radical decentralization,* a term I have coined for the purpose of making my points.

As a businessman I am just sick and tired of the waste—not only waste of opportunities and money, but the more tragic waste of the people who are managers—that our present highly centralized forms of management create.

What right have I to put forth a concept as radical as the one I am proposing here?

Let me say that I have worked on all sides and at all levels of management. I have worked in the management of a small family-owned corporation, and as a senior executive of one of the country's largest corporations. I've operated businesses on a radically decentralized basis (with a high degree of success, I might add), and I have tried to work successfully in a centralized management environment.

All my education and experience have been in business. Whether working as the boss or as a hired hand, I have always thought of myself as an entrepreneur. I have always tried to keep an open mind and look for not only what is right with the way we are doing things but also what can be improved.

There is a great deal that can be improved in the way we are doing business in America. Under our present systems we are destroying one of our greatest resources, our managers.

We are taking all the fun and pleasure—and, therefore, the

motivation—out of productive management work. Our big companies in particular have become almost socialistic in the policies and practices they establish for their management employees—and thus provide precious little in the way of opportunity for personal development.

Worst of all, America is getting its pants kicked off by foreign competitors, many of which are smart enough to let their managers manage.

If this book were to have its ultimate effect, the management people throughout the United States would rise up in rebellion, stand up for their rights, and refuse any longer to play the role of "naughty children" for "big daddy" back at headquarters.

If American business continues its self-destruction through its current practices of management centralization, we will end up with no managers in the future, and no one willing to become a manager. Our country's enterprises will be run by a few tired old men in the ivory towers of giant corporations who will run "their" businesses and our lives almost solely on the basis of what they understand from reading computer printouts.

The rest of us will be automatons.

Robert E. Levinson

Contents

Introduction:
A Time for Revolution

Business should be fun for two very good reasons. The first is that you spend so much of your time there. The second is that, as everyone knows, the more enjoyable an activity is, the better you do it.

Business *can* be fun—and simultaneously more profitable—if you make it fun. Fun lies with achievement and the risk that goes with achievement. Business is fun when you see something being created before your own eyes and know you played an important role in creating it. It's fun when you build an organization of six people or 60 or 6,000 and watch it become worthwhile and strong. It's fun when you see people develop and know you had a hand in their development. It's fun when you are put to the test of meeting hard challenges, making tough decisions, and solving thorny problems that stump other managers, and can take pride in the way you respond.

Business is fun when you experience the thrill of figuring out a better way to get the job done, take a chance on one of your people and see him come through, persuade a hard-nosed prospect that his road to profits lies in doing business with you. It's fun when you watch an idea you conceived as a faltering embryo take on muscle and brawn and achieve its objective in life. It's fun when you know that something is working because *you* made it work. It's fun, and it's profitable too.

1

My Own Experience with Centralized Business

Steelcraft Manufacturing Company, a family-owned business founded by my father and brother, started with an idea and a handful of people. Over the years it grew into the nation's leading producer of steel doors and frames for industrial and commercial use—and a host of other products as well. For many years after my father died, I served as the company's president and had a hand in its growth. I shared in the pride and joy of achievement. I helped Steelcraft maintain and sustain its high place in the market and had one helluva good time in the process.

AN EXTENDED HONEYMOON

About ten years ago Steelcraft merged with American Standard Corporation and I became a group vice president of the parent company. We were now in the Big Time, and I looked forward to the experience. At long last I could enjoy the perquisites many corporate executives take for granted: centralized staff service, good compensation plans, the pleasant "club" atmosphere, the increased personal status we all seek, whether we admit it or not. Or so I thought.

I lasted ten years at American Standard, about seven of them interesting and enjoyable, two or three quite frustrating.

To set the record straight and help you appreciate the perspective from which this book is written, let me make it clear at the outset that mine is a nonfinancial background. At Steelcraft my responsibilities were those of running the business and meeting the payroll on a week-to-week and month-to-month basis. I dealt with suppliers and customers and negotiated with distributors. I was involved in myriad problems and decisions, ranging from sales and engineering to production and product development. I set company policies and altered them when necessary. I hired and fired key people. I spent a major portion of my time working with and communicating with people. I spent relatively little time working with numbers. We had experts for that.

My early years at American Standard provided a good deal of the fun and excitement I had anticipated. But those years were unusual. My experience with this large corporation didn't become typical until much later on. You see, I was born and raised in the building industry and, for one thing, retained the presidency of Steelcraft as well as being group vice president for American Standard. For another thing, most of the companies I worked with as "the guy from the New York office" were in the same industry. At one point I was responsible for as many as eight separate companies, including my old company. Needless to say, those companies were essentially successful and profitable, or I wouldn't have lasted a year, let alone ten.

What made the situation unique, and for me enjoyable, was that I operated as a "group executive" for American Standard pretty much as I'd operated as chief executive of Steelcraft. I worked with the presidents of the divisions on a kind of partnership arrangement, working *with* them, not at them. I helped them with problems, policies, and programs when they expressed the need to be helped, didn't plague them with a lot of numbers, and in the main left them alone. That's where the big difference comes in. In a very real sense, all these divisions were radically decentralized even though they were under the aegis of a group executive from headquarters. Call it de facto radical decentralization.

Another thing I'd like to make clear is that I have no ax to grind with American Standard. The company has some very fine, outstanding people. I have always had a great deal of respect for the company and many of the top executives, and I still do. Any negative statements or implications directed against corporate meddling, obfuscation, or dehumanization made in this book are not leveled against American Standard in particular but against centralized corporations in general. My guess is that American Standard is neither less nor more typical than most of them.

The reason I was successful at American Standard, my divisions were successful, and I had fun doing my job was that a hands-off policy was applied to me as a group vice president, just as I applied a hands-off policy in dealing with the divisions. And the two reasons I was left alone were, as I said, that the operations were profitable and, equally important, that American Standard fell into hard times back in 1970 and deep trouble over a period of years.

When I sold my company for stock, shares of American Standard were selling at about $39. About a year later the stock fell to approximately $7 a share, and for a while it was a breath-holding game, with chief-executive anxieties centered around the possibilities of bankruptcy. I became one of nine group vice presidents at the time; we all worked very hard, and we pulled the company through. But I can tell you that top management had neither the time nor the poor judgment to shove the corporate finger into my pie. So I enjoyed a kind of independence and entrepreneurial freedom that is almost unheard of in centralized corporations—and this includes almost all big corporations.

BACK TO BUSINESS, CENTRALIZED STYLE

It was only after the company weathered the storm and became profitable again that it reverted to type. Top management had a lot of things on its mind and wanted to make the corporation prosper and grow. It decided to reorganize the company and place four senior vice presidents in charge of the group vice presidents. I was required to report to one of these men, and for the first time came to realize what it means to function as a genuine group vice president. This was difficult for me, as it is for most executives who have an operations background. The problem I faced was that I was accustomed to "doing my thing" in my own renegade nonconformist way, and making money in the process—and suddenly I was confronted with a superior who told me, "No, that's not the way I want things done." I made money for the company, but my style was not the company's style.

Well, that's the way I knew from experience things *had* to be done for the operation to be profitable. You see, even though I was absorbed into the Big Corporation, I didn't stop being a businessman, and I couldn't stop *thinking* like a businessman. When I balked at being anything else, when I refused to conform, I was fired.

After I left, my replacement, following the senior vice president's instructions, spent thousands of dollars restructuring the company and putting in a whole lot of "reforms." Now, from the latest word along the grapevine, Steelcraft has been restructured again to the way it was before it was restructured the first time. The "reforms" were for the main part discontinued. The operation is beginning to be successful again, and everybody is happy—for the time being at least.

The Lesson I Learned under Centralized Management

My experience as a group executive taught me a great deal and reinforced some things I already knew. The sum and substance of this knowledge, which I regard as vitally important to the U.S. economy in general and to every ambitious executive and would-be executive in particular, is presented as the concept of radical decentralization set forth in this book. Not merely decentralization—a management philosophy to which varying degrees of lip service are paid by many corporations—but genuine, honest-to-goodness *radical decentralization* (RD).

In a nutshell, the RD I have in mind is a return to the kind of entrepreneurism that made this country great. It is not the "art" or "science" of management, but the *process* of management by which a business or part of a business is managed by people who live and work on the scene on a day-to-day basis. It is management—which includes major decision making and problem solving—by men and women who have a deep, personal stake in the enterprise. It is management by the manager who is accustomed to meeting a payroll week in and week out. It is not remote-control management by a numbers juggler or "management scientist," sitting in an ivory tower a thousand miles away from the business, who never met a payroll in his life.

RD is as compellingly beneficial as numbers-oriented centralization is compellingly detrimental, as each chapter of this book will make increasingly clear. But the most compelling RD plus of all is the human plus. I have seen it time and again in company after company and division after division. Given two potentially profitable enterprises and two intelligent qualified managers, the operation that will flourish and grow is almost inevitably the one that is run by the operating executive on the scene; the one most likely to fail—or not live up to potential—is the one that is run by the remote-control manager, however smart and well trained he might be. And the dominant reasons are almost invariably human reasons.

5

Radical decentralization does not guarantee success. Only good management, savvy and sensitive management, and favorable market conditions can do that. But RD multiplies the *likelihood* of success by a factor of ten, whereas centralized management substantially reduces it.

In the radically decentralized company I am talking about, the operation is completely autonomous. A management team is in charge at the premises. The top executive is called president, the men and women who work with him vice presidents. So long as overall organizational goals are adhered to and the operation is profitable, they run their own show. They hire the people they want, select the marketing strategies they think will be successful, choose the suppliers from which they feel they will get the best deal, and advertise where and when their experience and judgment tell them it will be most effective.

The executive team is in charge. It knows it is in charge. Its employees know it is in charge. The community knows the executives are in charge. You don't run into the kind of situation I saw in one Cincinnati company that's so typical of thousands of other companies across the country. The division of the major corporation I'm referring to had in excess of 10,000 employees. The man in charge is a "division manager." The key people working under him are mainly supervisors or department heads.

What's wrong with this setup? Simply this. Down the street from this operation is a small company with 76 employees that is run by a president and three vice presidents. If you don't think this makes a difference, you don't know human nature. So far as the community is concerned, so far as the centralized company's number-one man is concerned, so far as his relatives, neighbors, and friends are concerned, he's *only* a division manager. He's responsible for 10,000 people and millions of dollars of business, and he's only a manager. So what? Does it bother him? You're damn right it does. And he put it quite bluntly: "It eats at my craw!" No wonder. The guy who runs an operation well under one-hundredth the size of his enjoys more status than he does. Not only that, the president of the 76-person company makes his own decisions and calls his own shots. My friend, the division manager, has to double-check with the brass back in New York if he wants an extra key made for the men's room. Well, not quite, but you get the idea.

"FIDDLE-FADDLE"

Do you know what I'm talking about? I'm talking about the so-called human factor, the problems, frustration, and bitterness triggered by depersonalization and dehumanization. When I attempted to persuade some of the corporate money boys that executives on the scene are turned off and dehumanized by remote proxy management, I got back funny looks. The looks said, hey, come on, you're old-fashioned, you're not with it, you're not riding the bandwagon.

They were right. I never was a bandwagon rider. I like to think of myself as a businessman. Well, I learned something I shall never forget. One great difference between the centralized corporation and the RD corporation boils down to a matter of values and focus. The big-money-numbers boys, it turned out, couldn't care less about what the division guys and gals think, what the public thinks, what the community thinks.

They spelled it out in so many words as "fiddle-faddle." They called it insignificant. "It's not the key to running a business. The key is how well we position our debt to equity and to capital expenditures, how we position our margins, what we do with our debentures, how we handle our overall strategy plans."

Who cares what a division manager thinks? It's what Wall Street thinks that counts.

I couldn't have disagreed more. In my experience, managing a business is synonymous with managing people. Manage people successfully and your business will be well managed. I tried to argue and reason with those guys, but there was no meeting of minds. There was, therefore, a parting of ways. When you discount the feelings and opinions of your people, I've learned, you sell them short, not only as human beings but as managers as well. You sell short their brains, experience, motivational self-interest, and intuitive judgment.

There's a story about a presumably learned meteorologist, a scientist if you will, who reports the weather for a major television network. One day shortly before he was due on the air he ran into the studio porter.

"It's gonna rain," the porter said.

7

The weatherman smiled indulgently. "No way! There's no rain in sight."

"It's gonna rain," the other insisted.

"I checked my telescope and instruments. It can't rain."

"It's gonna rain."

Exasperated, the scientist asked, "How do you know?"

"My corns hurt."

P.S.: it rained. Know something? Sometimes you have to go by your corns. Sometimes gut feeling based on experience is worth more than all the formulas and statistics your researchers and mathematicians could come up with.

I think we have to pay more attention to the gut managers in our business and social establishments, the men and women who know what they're doing, not because the charts tell them so, but because they've been doing it for years and they know that it works. I give computers their due. I give the management scientists their due. But let's not trade in the brains, experience, and hard-won intuitive judgment for a bunch of statistical printouts.

This is precisely what the centralized companies seem to be doing too often. And people are being de-peopled as a result. Managers are being reduced to half-managers. It's one thing to have Daddy tell you what to do and how to do it when you're a child. That's the learning process. It's another thing to have to lean on Daddy for important decisions and moves when you're an adult. That's the dehumanization process. It deprives you of the joy of accomplishment. Instead of building self-confidence, it saps it. It is ego-erosive. In short, it takes the fun out of business.

Comes the Revolution

I think I can safely predict that in the years ahead there will be mounting dissatisfaction with proxy corporate management by people who in a very real sense are being subjected to a kind of occupational emasculation. It is happening already at all levels of employment. In 1979 the Communications Workers of America, which represents 484,000 American Telephone & Telegraph Company employees, launched a nationwide advertising campaign in which the ads proclaimed: "Everybody has a boiling point. We are people, not machines."

Nor is the rebellion confined to rank-and-filers. Not so long ago hundreds of supervisors employed by a major Pittsburgh steel manufacturer formed a de facto union under the guise of a supervisors' social club. The avowed objective: to come up with ways and means to get management to treat them like human beings and give them the responsibility, authority, and voice they regard as essential to conducting their jobs most effectively.

A few years back the American Management Associations conducted a survey* to determine how its members felt about the unionization of managers. It was anticipated that only a small number would speak out in favor. Anything but. Nearly half the line executives responding said they would welcome a change in the labor laws that would force employers to bargain with managerial unions. This is merely one indication that when the entrepreneurial spirit is undermined, managers shift from a "we" to an "us against them" mentality. As Paul Parker once wrote: "What we picture ourselves to be, we become."

Proxy management, centralized to the hilt, pictures managers as mindless, unfeeling robots. Inevitably, when human beings are treated that way, frustrated and humiliated, they tend to wallow in bitterness and rebel.

As computerization continues to proliferate in our society, the temptation is strong to base decisions and business strategies more on printouts than on the experience-based brains-and-gut feelings of managers. More moves are remotely commandeered on the basis of grids than on grit. Increasing numbers of operating executives are occupationally emasculated. Impersonalization and dehumanization sap pride, achievement—and fun—from managerial jobs.

It is, I think, time for a change. Individuality and the free, independent entrepreneurial spirit are what made America great. Computerized, numbers-oriented, grid-directed centralization is currently challenging this inspiring heritage. It is time to face up to the challenge.

---

*Dale Tarnowieski, *The Changing Success Ethic: An AMA Survey Report.* New York: AMACOM, 1973.

PART I

What Is
Radical
Decentralization?

CHAPTER 1

Radical Decentralization: How It Works

There are good reasons to believe that the bright light of radical decentralization will shine upon increasing numbers of thoughtful businesspeople as the 1980s move on toward the 1990s. In these times a progressive executive could not help but ponder the adverse dehumanizing effects of pervasive automation and numbers orientation, despite the remarkable strides of the computer and its immense value as a management tool. Smart managers emulate and try to duplicate business success, and today they are getting more and more models to emulate.

A Look at Some Winners

An outstanding, if not the most notable, model is Beatrice Foods Company, a $3 billion Chicago-based conglomerate whose net earnings have steadily ascended with no fall-backs from about $1 million in 1953 to approximately $300 million today. "Decentralized profit-center management and strong financial controls are at the heart of our management philosophy," stated a full-page Beatrice Foods ad in *The Wall Street Journal*. The ad was headlined: "Why Companies That Join Beatrice Often Perform Better Than They Did Before." The copy went on to say:

> There are three good reasons. One is that the companies we acquire have access to the financial resources of a parent with

13

about $3 billion in total assets. Another is that we help them set their sights higher. And a third reason is that our companies can draw upon the knowledge and experience of their sister companies.

Beyond that, we leave them alone. Because we've learned that autonomy can best enable profit-center managers to respond quickly to changing operating environments, market conditions, and opportunities.*

Another enthusiastic exponent of radical decentralization is resource-equipment manufacturer E. H. "Hubie" Clark, head of Baker International Corporation, whose unprecedented 34 percent annual gains for each year during the past decade evoke gasps of admiration from envious competitors.

Here is how Clark spells out the guidelines by which his divisions will operate:

Each company will lay its own strategy, publish its own annual report, and, ultimately, even make acquisitions without parental approval. One reason is to breathe entrepreneurial spirit into division managers, who have become the new presidents of semi-autonomous companies. . . . They can say, "Those tracks in the sand are mine, not Hubie Clark's." †

Another conglomerate whose top management has the vision to appreciate the value of permitting divisional entrepreneurs to "do their own thing" is Cincinnati's Eagle-Picher Industries, Inc., whose acquired companies are into a host of products ranging from rubber goods and chemicals to gasoline-service equipment and rubber-processing machinery. Comments a Wall Street observer: "The destifling of the kind of pioneering spirit and entrepreneurship that made this nation great is a much needed and fast growing trend. This company appears to be catching on early and will be enjoying the fruits of the harvest."

Another corporation that seems to be catching on fast is $500-million-plus Tandem Computers, Inc. Tandem has shown growth of 100 percent annually over the past five years and, from a humble start, is now producing sales of $100 million per year. One reason for its progress and growth, according to some industry watchers, is its ability to attract high-caliber

---

* *The Wall Street Journal,* May 1, 1980.
†*Business Week,* April 28, 1980.

employees who stay. And the reason they stay is that they are treated like people, not robots.

"When you get above $5 million," concedes Gene M. Amdahl, founder and chairman emeritus of Amdahl Corporation, "it's hard for a person to manage everything like a mother hen. As the company grows, it's easy to lose the entrepreneur's vision of what the company should be. But I don't believe it absolutely has to happen."*

Neither does James G. Treybig, Tandem's cofounder and president, who contends that his company will need "its people-oriented management philosophy more than the latest technology to continue to grow at its current pace." One high payoff of this kind of advanced thinking is that the company has been able to attract and, as we said, *keep* outstanding managers in a geographical area where they are supposedly very difficult to come by.

Then we have West Germany's Bertelsmann Corporation publishing empire, piloted by Reinhard Mohn, who is known as "The King of Gutersloh" in the small Westphalian town his family long has dominated. Bertelsmann, once an obscure publisher of religious books, has invaded the United States and today generates revenues just a hair short of Time Inc.'s.

Mohn rules on investments, but steers clear of operations and, according to *Business Week,* sees himself as the company's "conductor" rather than its creative director. His philosophy: to leave implementation to the autonomous operating chiefs—so long as they perform. As the *Business Week* article states, he believes in "no more cooperation than exists in the free market." Fearing that committees would kill the entrepreneurial spirit of aggressive managers, Mohn keeps each of his operations separate. Or, as one of his chief aides puts it, "Each arm (of Bertelsmann) is a very independent kingdom."†

This philosophy augurs, I believe, a definite trend that is already gathering momentum in sager quarters of management. Kingdom or fiefdom—the distinction can make all the difference in the world: in building, boosting, and motivating key people; in humanizing an operation and promoting productivity improvement; and in attracting and retaining tal-

Business Week, July 14, 1980.
†*Business Week,* June 9, 1980.

ented managers. The reasons will be made clear in this and following chapters.

"Other Men's Porridge"

I never thrust my nose into other men's porridge. It is no bread and butter of mine; every man for himself and God for us all.

Miguel de Cervantes, *Don Quixote de la Mancha*

I strongly believe that in the foreseeable future a significant measure of corporate success will be the degree to which top management refrains from thrusting its nose into the porridge of the companies and divisions spawned and acquired by the parent. I would not want any reader to labor under the mistaken notion that I'm opposed to acquisitions and mergers. Quite the contrary. I think the acquisition-bent corporation stands to enjoy a uniquely favorable opportunity in this particular era of American business if its head honchos are genuinely and honestly of a mind to keep their noses pointed windward to financial-support activities and the realistic evaluation of performance against projected expectations and well away from the day-to-day activities of the operating divisions.

The evidence is already starting to build. A major reason Beatrice Foods Co. was able to woo and win such outstanding companies as Samsonite, Peter Eckrich & Sons, Culligan, and Day-Timers is because of the image and reputation the parent developed for keeping its corporate nose out of the boondocks.

Notes a prominent Wall Street analyst: "In my view the company's success to date is largely attributable to its hands-off hands-on philosophy. In a nutshell, management believes the hands-on executive is best qualified to make the subsidiary's key business decisions, and so long as results are acceptable, the parent's executives are best advised to adhere to a hands-off policy."

I know of one radically decentralized corporation where, after acquiring a well-rated company, one of the first things the parent's chief executive does is to assure the division's president that he's happy with the way things are going. "It's your baby," he says, "to nurse along as you see fit. We won't interfere so long as objectives are met."

16

The trouble, of course, is that many acquiring corporations give such assurance—and only time can reveal their degree of sincerity. But in this operation, the president of the newly merged division and some of his key aides are given "good faith" salary boosts. They could receive no better convincer. Notes one president: "You don't raise a manager's salary if your intention is to curtail his powers and make an order taker out of him."

The Basic Recipe

Four central features distinguish the radically decentralized company from the centralized corporation:

1. Its divisions are independent entrepreneurial units, headed by presidents, under the corporate umbrella. The parent company's role is primarily that of a banker for its operating divisions.

2. The organization is thoroughly humanized—that is, decisions are based not just on financial parameters and computer printouts but on human factors as well.

3. Decisions are made by hands-on managers ("experts") at the scene rather than by headquarters numbers men ("specialists") far removed from the actual operation.

4. There is an ongoing effort to thwart the natural tendency toward bureaucratization and to keep the organization lean and flexible for fast and effective decision making.

Let's take a closer look now at these ingredients of radical decentralization.

Autonomy of the Entrepreneurial Unit

Under RD, all decisions affecting the operation of a division, including diversification within the limits of the basic business, are made by the divisional managers, who are accountable to corporate top management for final results but not for operational details. By the same token, all decision making within the unit is continuously pushed as far down the line as possible. In other words, under RD, managers are allowed—and expected—to be managers, not merely policemen enforcing decisions made at the chessboard by headquarters specialists.

17

In particular, the decentralized unit is not tied into any central computer system, corporate insurance program, corporate salary and benefits administration plan, corporate purchasing program, corporate marketing and sales program, corporate cash pool, or corporate R&D program. Furthermore, each unit has sole responsibility for all hiring and training, all patent-law matters, and all labor-relations problems except as dictated by national labor contracts. Finally, if there is a corporate consulting group, it must *sell* its services to the divisions in open competition with outside specialists.

Entrepreneurial independence of the operating divisions guards against the imposition of inappropriate corporate standards and procedures on the local units, thus keeping decision making responsive to local needs, problems, and opportunities. By contrast, decisions in the centralized corporation must pass through a multilayered channel of authorization, often resulting in missed opportunities and escalation of problems to the point of crisis.

Focusing the decision power at the local level also makes it easier for management to pay attention to "little" issues that would seem insignificant, in terms of the money involved, to the headquarters specialist but that are in fact critical for the survival of the operation. A case in point is a wage-increase demand by the local union that appears modest compared with corporate standards but that is totally out of line with regional or industry standards and would seriously jeopardize the economic viability of the division.

THE PARENT COMPANY'S ROLE UNDER RD

Under radical decentralization, corporate headquarters provides three basic functions for the corporation at large and for its operating divisions:

1. It furnishes the stockholders who own equity in the organization.
2. It furnishes the board of directors.
3. It serves as a bank for the corporation at large and its operating divisions.

It is the banking, or treasury, function and how it is implemented that marks the essential difference between the typically centralized corporation and the radically decentralized organization. Under RD, the corporation fulfills pretty much the same role as a bank.

Let us say, for example, that you want to start a doughnut manufacturing business and go to the bank for a loan to get the enterprise under way. The bank's loan officer would want to know how much money you want, why you want the money, and how you are planning to use it. He would want to make sure you were a responsible businessperson of sound mind, that your plan was basically feasible, and that you had the experience and know-how necessary to start a business in general and a doughnut business in particular. He would not want to know if the doughnuts you plan to make would be sugar-coated or glazed, if they would be filled with jelly or custard, how much they would sell for, who your customers would be, where you would buy your materials and how much you would pay for them, or how big the damned holes will be. That's *your* business. If you don't know that, you have no right to open a plant.

The radically decentralized corporation would serve the same role as a bank, with a few minor additions. As president of the operating division, you would submit a budget to corporate headquarters, along with the balance sheet and the profit-and-loss statement you would give a bank as a going concern. The corporation's financial vice president would want to know how much money you need, what you need it for, and what return on investment you expect. If you were getting the basic desired *results* month to month and year to year, that's about all he would want to know. How you dot your i's and cross your t's would be of little importance to him.

FINANCIAL REPORTING AND CONTROLS

Needless to say, under RD or any other concept, a certain degree of standardization or conformity would be necessary. The corporate financial vice president would develop the reporting formats and techniques that are most comfortable and convenient for him. Uniformity of the books of the total corporation would have to be achieved in line with tax and legal requirements. Periodic reviews and presentations would be necessary.

But they would be capsulized or summary reviews that are results-oriented rather than line-item-oriented, and therein lies the big difference between the remotely managed organization and the RD corporation. In the centralized operation, the division manager is summoned to corporate headquarters every so often for an "in-depth review." Typically, you'll have 25 corporate executives in the room with you, staff nitpickers who never had to meet a payroll. You'll have a marketing guy, a planning expert, a research genius, an economist, a personnel specialist, a couple of accountants, a half-dozen or so assorted financial types, a computer expert, and heaven only knows what else.

These people will sit and listen to you expound about your operation like drama critics called in to review a tottering Broadway production. At these pot-shot meetings, the experts will want to know why your research-and-development costs are up, why you need so much money for advertising, why you haven't raised the price of product line B, why the personnel manager needs an assistant for $19,000 a year, why certain items that aren't showing a profit are being kept in the line.

This session alone costs thousands of dollars—an entourage of headquarters experts, plus key people from the division flown in, hoteled, and fed. The payoff? Humiliated division managers, who learn once more that their job is to execute orders, not to make decisions.

PLANNING

Overkill in planning can be worse than seat-of-the-pants management. When a corporation has a planning and strategy department, as most big companies do, much of the authority to plan is taken out of the unit. In spite of that, a great deal of duplication occurs.

One of the divisions for which I was responsible as a group vice president was Steelcraft Manufacturing. There was no "planning department" at Steelcraft, but one manager was in charge of formulating and documenting the company's plan. This executive's job was to spell out what Steelcraft was going to do next week, next month, and next year, how it was going to be done, what the company hoped to accomplish. That was step one.

Step two was for me, as group vice president, to review the plan with Steelcraft's manager.

My boss at American Standard was a senior vice president,

and he had a planning manager working for him. Step three was for this manager to go over the plan, request information where he felt it was warranted, and suggest changes if he considered them necessary.

From that point, believe it or not, the plan was shunted to corporate headquarters with its centralized planning department. Step four was for this body of experts to review the planning to date and add its six cents to the kitty.

Well, I can tell you, by the time the damn thing got all cooked through, salted, and spiced, and chopped up, we had nothing much left but a hodge-podge of numbers, and the task now was to juggle the numbers and make them come out the way the experts thought they ought to come out. More often than not that was as far removed from the original plan formulated at the unit in line with division goals, aspirations, and needs as the Gulf of Mexico is from Sydney, Australia.

However you slice it, it simply doesn't make sense. I had been born into Steelcraft. Pints of my life blood went into that company. I knew the business as well as the service-station guy on the corner knows the business he owns. And damn it, when I ran it Steelcraft was highly successful and chalked up a nice respectable profit year after year. I was the guy on the scene, and knew what I was doing when I planned. In fact, I planned so well that American Standard acquired the business! From almost any point of view I can conjure up, if the unit's plan is working successfully, the smartest thing headquarters can do is refrain from tampering with it.

But under centralization, if you don't tamper, you're not earning your keep.

Under radical decentralization, instead of a 14-layer cake, you wind up with a simple single-layer cake that is highly digestible. The corporation's president and board of directors set specific goals in terms of earnings expectations and return on investment that establish the division's general direction and purpose. Some organizations want high returns in a hurry; others want a good return but are willing to develop it gradually over the longer pull. One board decides the division should zero in on growth opportunities in a volatile environment; another opts for steady performance in a stable market.

Questions are thrashed out and resolved with regard to the degree of risk the corporation is willing to take, general policy pertaining to product-line scope, and acquisitions. Once overall goals are established, the corporation's president goes to the president of the division, gives him the goals you decided on, and gets his agreement that they are realistic and fair. From that point on the president's and division's fortunes rise or fall on his achievement or lack of achievement. Now, with his work cut out for him, the president of the unit hammers out an overall plan with his top strategy people and submits it to the corporate chief.

If the unit's plan requires a budget of $12 million and the chief insists $10 million is as high as the corporation will go, it is now the unit head's responsibility to come up with a viable alternative plan in line with the budget requirement. Like the original plan, the alternative plan is worked out by people within the division. It doesn't go through the corporate planning mill, where layers upon layers of numerologists and computer experts wield their axes at will and with little if any true understanding of the division's problems and needs.

THE LIMITS OF FREEDOM

Radical decentralization by itself is no guarantee of business success. Success ultimately depends on the quality of the people managing the operation. If management is incompetent, the financial results will soon make it evident, especially under RD, where managers make real decisions with measurable financial consequences and do not simply carry out remotely engineered decisions for which nobody claims full and clear responsibility.

It is in such cases—when performance fails to measure up to preestablished and agreed-upon levels—that intervention by the corporate parent must be considered. Danger signals include:

- Sales volume significantly below forecast, with expenses not reflecting the lower volume.
- Loss of market share (poor pricing, distribution, or product?).
- Cash-flow problems (slow receivables).
- Exceptionally high employee turnover.
- Too high a proportion of capital-equipment expenditures incurred during the earlier parts of the budget period (indicating the possibility of a significant budget overrun).
- Below-standard R&D expenditures (danger of obsolescence).

If any of these conditions occur, corporate management has no choice but to investigate the causes and, where necessary, intrude its managerial presence. In some cases, where fully competent division management is lacking, it may mean a temporary return to centralization until strong management teams are developed that make a decentralized approach likely to succeed. Thus I present radical decentralization not as a panacea for an ailing enterprise, or as a guarantee of business success, but as the concept of management under which humanization, personalization, *and maximum profit results* are most readily achieved, given a people-sensitive management team and the right set of circumstances.

The Human Factor

One day Delta Airlines mechanic Jim Burnett found his paycheck $38 short. There was an error in his overtime calculation for the day he had come in at 2 A.M. to repair an L-1011 engine. When he showed his check to his supervisor, he was put off and couldn't get satisfaction. So he wrote a letter to David C. Garrett, Jr., Delta's president, and complained about the pay situation in general and his own problem in particular. The result: (1) prompt payment of the money due, (2) an apology from top management, (3) a change in the payment procedure. The cardinal sin of going over your supervisor's head? It's no sin at Delta.

Notes Janet Guyon in *The Wall Street Journal:*

> Such reaction from top executives to the little problems of Delta's 36,500 employees isn't an isolated incident. It's part of a sophisticated personnel policy to maintain what Delta calls its best asset: an unusually productive and loyal work force. The strategy, which includes virtual open-door access for all employees to top management, has kept Delta largely non-union and made it a consistent money-maker in an industry plagued with labor-management strife.*

The management philosophy that encourages personalized attention to employee needs and complaints is referred to as "the Delta family feeling." Its main theme is that the company cares. Does the policy pay off? In spades and more. In a trou-

* *The Wall Street Journal,* July 7, 1980.

23

ble-ridden industry, not only has Delta been consistently profitable, but it has consistently and successfully countered Transport Workers of America's efforts to organize it.

The key to Delta's success is that its caring policy goes a long way beyond the lip service so many large corporations pay the philosophy of showing employees they count. A prime example occurred in 1973 when the oil embargo prompted most other airlines to announce heavy layoffs. Delta refused to follow suit. Chairman W. Thomas Beebe told senior managers: "Now the time has come for the stockholders to pay a little penalty for keeping the team together."

The penalty, time proved, was a small investment in bigger dividends to come. Few people quit at Delta, and it's hard to find employees with serious complaints. One reason employee satisfaction is high is that the company goes to great pains to screen and hire job applicants. The conclusion speaks for itself: when you employ superior people, you have to treat them in a superior way to keep them happy and productive, and in order to keep them, period.

The human touch, however minutely evidenced, counts for much with Delta management. Uniforms for its 6,000 stewards and stewardesses, for example, are selected by a committee of flight attendants. Mechanics even choose their immediate supervisors.

Yet the company is anything but lax and permissive. It sets high standards of training and performance and expects employees to abide by them. And it guards its image zealously. Last year it fired a flight attendant for exposing her rear end in *Playboy* magazine, clearly an action out of keeping with Delta's "family feeling."

HUMANIZED MANAGEMENT: A NATURAL BY-PRODUCT OF DECENTRALIZATION

Don't misunderstand me. An ess-oh-bee who switches jobs from a centralized to a decentralized corporation will still in all likelihood be an ess-oh-bee. Decentralization doesn't change a person's character if he is naturally dishonest, greedy, or selfish. But, for one thing, it helps a manager *avoid* becoming dishonest, greedy, and selfish. And for another, it makes humanization easy and natural.

Take Ben Farrel (name disguised), for example. Ben is 60

24

years old. A sales rep employed by a successful medium-size decentralized company, he was for ten years or so ranked among the top 25 percent of income producers. If the company retired him at full pay tomorrow, it would still be well ahead of the game. In his time Ben wrote millions of dollars of business and contributed significantly to his employer's enviable position in the marketplace.

When he was in his thirties, forties, and early fifties, the rep was what could be described as an aggressive and dynamic go-getter. Hungry and ambitious, he put everything he had into the job and maybe a little bit more. Today at 60 he's comfortably fixed—but not independently wealthy—and admittedly no longer interested in conquering the world. He's slowed down so that his boss, the sales manager, is understandably concerned that Ben is no longer getting full potential out of his choice urban territory.

Okay, you get the picture, I'm sure. It was drawn with a very specific purpose in mind: to illustrate a significant difference between the typical centralized and decentralized company. In the centralized company, Ben Farrel would be an income-and-expense factor in an operation located a thousand or so miles from corporate headquarters. One day the computer would alert management to the fact that his performance had slipped, that he was no longer getting the expected yield from his accounts, and, after a couple of warnings to shape up, he would—nervous and anxiety-ridden by this time—probably be fired.

In the decentralized well-run organization, Ben Farrel would be a hell of a lot more than an income-and-expense factor. He would be a savvy and highly qualified pro who spent the best years of his life working for the company, had made an exceptionally good accounting of himself, and, what's more, had made some strong, lasting friendships among his colleagues, customers, and superiors. Faced with the problem of what to do about Ben, his superior would probably find some way to adjust to his advancing age and changing lifestyle requirements. He might chop a piece off his territory to give him less of a workload. Or he might bring him into the home office, if he seemed amenable to the idea, to work with young reps and new recruits to put his knowledge and years of experience to use and, at the same time, help Ben phase down reasonably and realistically without stripping him of his status and self-respect in the process.

In short, Ben would be regarded as a person, a flesh-and-blood human being, not as a factor which, superficially, adds or subtracts from the company's bottom-line figure.

You become people-oriented in a business when your planning and strategies encompass not only stated corporate and divisional goals but human needs and aspirations as well. In dealing with people, you don't lose sight of organizational objectives. But you tie these objectives into individual values and entitlements, into such considerations as age, years of service, past contribution, and loyalty. And if you can match up human and organizational objectives and needs to achieve a balance that keeps people happy and productive, you wind up *earning* the loyalty and team spirit every corporation needs to flourish and grow, and you wind up keeping your good and talented people and attracting new top-notch people, because the relationship isn't one-sided—you're as loyal to them as they are to you.

TWO-WAY COMMUNICATION—THE WAY TO BUILD A TEAM

In recent years, states business writer Herbert E. Meyer, a lot of top executives have been discovering that communication is an art as well as a science. "Today," he says, "everyone understands clearly [an assertion I would question] that information has to flow in both directions in a large hierarchical organization." He goes on to say that just as famous experiments at Western Electric demonstrated some years ago, "employees want a sense of participation—a feeling that they are members of the team." *

With this last I couldn't agree more, and that's one of the big problems in the centralized organization. The yes men and instruction fulfillers at the divisions *aren't* part of the team. They don't *participate;* they routinely perform what they are told to perform. In place of a two-way flow, they get one-way mandates.

Unless you have experienced this personally, it is impossible to imagine how frustrating and emasculating the process

* *Fortune,* June 1975.

can be. At Steelcraft I used to have a rule that required all traveling salespeople to call in once a day. It gave them a chance to talk, let off steam, express themselves, get their ideas across, boast if they landed an important order, complain or cry if they missed one. Most of all I wanted them to know that someone back home *cared* about what they were doing and thinking, that their opinions were respected, that the job they did counted.

I think this kind of back-and-forth exchange is important, whether it's between a person in the field and a headquarters-based manager or a person in the division and a superior whose actions and reactions affect his day-to-day job and his future. And I think this is usually missing in the large centralized corporation.

SELF-ESTEEM VERSUS DEFLATION

Mark Twain once said, "I can live for two months on a good compliment."

It would be impossible to overstate the importance and value of occasional pats on the back, the assurance from others that "hey, you're doing a great job. You're important to me. You're important to the organization."

Compliments, honest flattery, ego massaging—they're nourishment for the mind and the heart. In his famous book, *I'm OK—You're OK,* Thomas A. Harris refers to it as "stroking." He writes, "Every child is stroked in the first year of life simply by the fact that he had to be picked up to be cared for. Without at least minimal handling the infant would not survive."* He goes on to point out in his book that stroking is essential to normal development as the individual progresses through childhood, young adult life, and maturity. It is where stroking is missing that the "not O.K." person develops. This is one of the basic tenets of Transactional Analysis.

Stroking takes a variety of forms during the individual's working life. One of its major manifestations, I think, relates to achievement. A manager makes a particularly good deal. A sales executive comes up with a program that is well received by the boss and the company's customers. A training manager devises a course that gets an enthusiastic response from em-

*New York: Harper & Row, 1969, p. 67.

ployees. A finance person works up an audit procedure that saves time and multiplies effectiveness. A manufacturing executive concocts a clever way to boost plant productivity. The organization's goal is to improve profits in all of these cases. But so far as the individual is concerned, it goes a lot deeper than that, and that's where the stroking comes in.

I can tell you from personal experience that it means a great deal to a person to come home to his spouse and announce, "Hey, sweetheart, do you know what I did today?" Or, "Remember that marketing plan I told you about? Well, the boss thinks it's terrific." Or, "They're putting my idea to cut rejects into effect." Or, "Do you know what the chief told me today . . .?"

Achievement! We all need it to feel needed, to feel important, to build and develop self-confidence, to stroke ourselves and get stroking from others. We need to win the plaudits of loved ones and associates.

Achievement is born out of *personal* effort expended, out of ideas thrashed out in the loneliness of our minds, out of decisions that turn out right. At the managerial level at least, achievement does *not* result, except on a limited basis, from routinely following instructions transmitted from remote decision centers.

When the desire to achieve is thwarted, it inevitably leads to frustration. If it happens often enough, it produces "not O.K." people. A typical centralized scenario might run something like this. A medium-size door company is taken over by a conglomerate. The initial response at the division level is enthusiasm. Finally, we're going to get the capital we need to grow and expand. Didn't Daddy, the banker, say this in so many words: "Let's put money into the company, let's win and maintain a larger share of the market, let's develop this enterprise into a big operation"? With the prospects bright, the people in the division, the ones who know the marketplace, who have lived and grown with the business, who understand the company's needs, see a change taking place in the industry. They get together, confer, and decide: "If we're to go along and stay ahead of the trend, we're going to have to market this door and frame as a package, with the hardware already on it, so that it can be installed as is right in the building. We

28

know this business, and we know that's what will have to be done. That means we're going to have to buy a company that makes hinges and locks. It's the only sensible way to do it, the only way to keep costs under control."

On the heels of this decision, the division people envision all kinds of profits and growth. They understand the situation; they know just what they're proposing.

They can almost smell the achievement potential and, although no one articulates it as such, sense the stroking that will inevitably follow success. The only thing that remains is to get Daddy's okay, and the financial support necessary, the support already taken for granted.

Of course you guessed the result. Daddy doesn't agree. In his infinite computer-based wisdom, he feels the idea is ill conceived, isn't cost-effective, or fits lopsidedly into the matrix.

End of idea. End of achievement. Divisional frustration sets in. In time, with repetition of blind rejection in response to ideas and proposals, frustration deepens. Decision paralysis takes over. Not O.K. managers stop managing and become managers in name only. They stop being men. They stop being women. They become disenfranchised clerks.

Which is by no means O.K., as Dr. Harris would put it.

Hands-On Management

I can tell you from hard-won experience that centralization, as practiced by most medium-large and large corporations, is a synonym for counterproductivity. One reason is that it stifles the individual growth and development of key managers and supervisors. It is human nature, unless one is encouraged to do otherwise, to tackle problems and decisions in the easiest and most risk-free way. Centralization, by removing authority and responsibility from the operating manager's shoulders, makes him dependent on the headquarters executives charged with overseeing the division.

Why is this counterproductive? Because nobody knows— or should know—better than the operating manager on the scene what decision or move would be in the division's best interests. And because, when fast action is needed, as is often the case, kicking the problem upstairs, with its communication delays and committee resolutions, can only delay action, compounding the problem or permitting opportunities to fade as the case may be.

I can recall one situation in a highly centralized New England company where a labor problem erupted on the heels of a headquarters-mandated compensation realignment. A committee of three appeared at the plant manager's desk to protest the change. He in turn shunted the problem to the division manager. He, in line with corporate practices and procedures, set up an appointment to discuss it with the parent company's labor-relations vice president.

He flew to Boston for this meeting. While there, he received a call from the plant. It had just gone out on strike. Ironically, the grievance at issue was a relatively simple one to resolve. Had the plant manager tackled the problem on the spot when it occurred and had a session or two with the grievants, the situation never would have gotten out of hand. The expensive communications, meetings, and strike would not have occurred; the financial cost would have been minimized.

I've seen it time and again. When layers of corporate management—corporate-suite theorists far removed from day-to-day operations—are put to work on division problems, the costs tend to proliferate along with the problems. Early in 1978, in an effort to dig to the root of battery-business erosion in its ESB Ray-O-Vac subsidiary, David C. Dawson, president of Inco Ltd., the Philadelphia-based parent, spent months talking with some 300 ESB managers. His prescription for positive restructuring following his intensive investigation: to eliminate layers of corporate supervision that were stifling the marketing of new battery products. Dawson's reorganization, in short, called for "a wholesale decentralization." Under the new arrangement ESB was divided into four clearly defined and fairly autonomous operating companies, and much greater responsibility was placed with operating managers. A major change involved product research and development, now conducted by the subsidiary. Under centralization, most R&D projects were clustered at a corporate technology center in Philadelphia. The new arrangement is expected to eliminate a pressing problem that made it hard for ESB to operate successfully in a fiercely competitive industry—an inability to bring new products to market quickly enough.

Noted a *Business Week* article:

> . . . each time, the yen for innovation was smothered either by the Byzantine bureaucracy or the overly cautious attitude at ESB's corporate headquarters. "Their technical people came up with ideas, but management didn't come out with the product," says Jerome T. Lawrie, a vice president at Chloride Inc., a Tampa (Fla.) battery company. "They maintained status quo, and now they are in the follower's position."*

Today the head of each ESB company has complete control over his operation and reports directly to Dawson.

THE CONFIDENCE FACTOR

One of the strongest arguments for radical decentralization is that it tends to promote independence and the initiative and the innovation this fosters. For productive innovation to occur, two vital ingredients are necessary: (1) self-confidence on the part of the manager, (2) faith and trust on the part of his boss.

RD tells a division manager, in effect: I believe you know better than any headquarters executive how your show should be run. You have my blessing, so go ahead and run it.

Centralization says: You're no more than a policeman and messenger boy. We'll call the shots here at headquarters. Your job is to follow instructions.

Under RD an executive has the power to execute. Under centralization, however politely, he's "told off." RD boosts a man's confidence. Centralization systematically undermines it. One of the chief problems in industry today is that 99 out of 100 chief executives, however highly centralized their organizations may be, will swear that they don't curb initiative. In my experience, 98 of them are mistaken.

The trouble is that while most managements profess to be in favor of independence and freedom, very few actually permit division executives to take action and make decisions on their own where major issues, or significant sums, are involved. They pay lip service to the concept, then apply fetters

---

Business Week, March 12, 1979.

when free movement is needed. Some chief executives go a half step beyond lip service, which could be worse than no step at all.

I talked with a division manager recently who told me the president of his parent company was outspoken in his conviction that for subsidiaries to function successfully, it was important that operating executives have the power and freedom to make critical spot decisions where called for without having to get headquarters approval. Although each division was under a group vice president's supervision, the VPs, reflecting the chief's policy and philosophy, were supposed to allow operating managers the leeway they needed to take independent unilateral action when the situation demanded it.

Conceptually, the arrangement sounds fine. Operationally, it only half worked. One day the manager had an opportunity to buy a product line from a competitor, along with certain equipment, materials, and facilities for producing it, all at a price he considered a steal. Not only was it a bargain; it also involved just the products needed to round out his own line. The manager told me, "I knew of at least two other competitors who would grab the deal if given half a chance. If I didn't make a spot decision and act right away, the opportunity could have slipped right through my fingers. We drew up an agreement then and there, and I issued a deposit check to confirm it."

Two days later the manager was at headquarters for a division strategy meeting. He told the group vice president about the deal he had made. The executive's face fell. He frowned and squirmed around in his chair. He finally said in an uncertain voice: "Yeah, I guess you know what you're doing."

An interpretation might read: "It was a damn fool thing to do. I disapprove of your hasty action without consulting me." Also implied in his attitude and tone was the threat: "Buddy, if this thing backfires, it's going to be your tail, not mine!"

Notes Harvard University Professor of Business Administration Richard F. Vancil: "Organizational climate is fundamentally determined by personal interactions among managers, that is, by how managers behave in those meetings and in the dozens of unscheduled informal contacts that they have with each other."*

Financial Executive, March 1980.

Proclaiming that you're all for independent action and initiative isn't enough. One has to act and live the part as well.

HANDS ON—PROFITS UP

I've seen it proved by case after case: when managers charged with calling the shots don't know the business, the operation suffers. International Paper Company, for example, is described as the nation's largest paper producer and landowner. If recent press reports are accurate, a great deal of upheaval and foment within the organization has been taking place over the last decade or so, with all kinds of strategic cost control and budget plans implemented.

According to some industry spokespeople, bottom-line results continue on the dismal side despite the many changes. In 1979, for example, a strong year for paper and wood products companies, *Business Week* reports, IP's operating earnings slipped 2.2 percent, compared with a 32 percent average increase for 17 other major forest-products companies. Whether chairman Edwin A. Gee, a recruit from Du Pont who took over the chief executive officer's chair in early 1980, can get the huge company wading down more profitable streams remains to be seen. But past woes, if the evaluation of industry watchers and competitors' key executives is accurate, are largely attributable to top-echelon inexperience. Remarked one: "International Paper is being run by a bunch of people who don't know the business."*

Not a paper-industry insider, I cannot vouch for this personally, but it smacks mightily of layerism and remote-control management. Notes a nationally known management consultant: "Companies are often stymied, not so much by the ineffectiveness of individual managers as by corporate organizational structure and policy." A euphemism for centralized management? Perhaps.

In a recently published book, *Making It in Management—the Japanese Way,* author Raymond Dreyfack writes:

> Mingle with the troops. Get to know them, what they are up to, and what kind of problems they're having. When the troops are strangers to you, strange things can happen. . . . Experience proves that the bigger the operation, the more ivory-

---

* *Business Week,* July 28, 1980.

tower management is apt to take place. One reason is that size tends to absorb excessive manpower and costs. If one employee fails to carry his weight in a five-person operation, it's apparent to all. When thousands of people and millions of dollars are involved, a host of carpets exist under which mistakes and waste can be swept. *

No company can develop the imagination, initiative, and creativity needed for top performance in today's fiercely competitive marketplace if it boxes in its key on-the-scene executives. In the well-managed organization, managers are imbued with the entrepreneurial spirit and encouraged to function with entrepreneurial spirit.

A recent *Business Week* article titled "Putting Excellence into Management" reports on a McKinsey Co. study of ten of the nation's best-managed corporations: International Business Machines, Texas Instruments, Hewlett-Packard, 3M, Digital Equipment, Procter & Gamble, Johnson & Johnson, McDonald's, Dana, and Emerson Electric. "On the surface," notes the writer, "they have nothing in common. There is no universality of product line: five are in high technology, one in packaged goods, one makes medical products, one operates fast-food restaurants, and two are relatively mundane manufacturers of mechanical and electrical products. But *each is a hands-on operator* [emphasis mine], not a holding company or a conglomerate." †

I don't know how many of these corporations are as radically decentralized as I would like them to be. But I think this is yet another indication of the trend taking place in America today—the one in which more and more thoughtful, profit-minded businesspeople are recognizing that remote-control management, however "advanced" or sophisticated it may be, can never match the effectiveness of on-the-scene experience, savvy, and gut feeling for the business.

The Antibureaucratic Organization

One of the major reasons for the inefficiency of large centralized corporations is their level of bureaucracy. The heart of the bureaucracy is the corporation's set of *standard operating*

*Farnsworth Publishing Co., 1982.
†July 21, 1980.

procedures, collected in a weighty, somber Corporate Policy Manual. The bureaucratic manager is nothing but a meticulous administrator of the company's standard operating procedures, which allow for no exception and replace creative thinking.

In the radically decentralized company, an ongoing effort is made to combat the natural tendency toward bureaucratization. Channels of communication are kept unclogged. Creative participation at all levels in problem solving is encouraged, using effective suggestion programs. All policies, procedures, and organizational structures are continuously questioned as to their contribution to the speed and flexibility of decision making. Use of the memo—the favorite time waster of the bureaucrat—is discouraged in favor of informal oral communication.

Perhaps the most powerful weapon against bureaucratization is the presence of direct channels for the "unusual"—those new ideas that just won't fit into the rule book. Bureaucracy thrives where there is a spirit of conformism. Where top management encourages nonconformism and gets employees at all levels involved in problem solving and decision making, a clean fresh wind will keep the bureaucracy out.

CHAPTER 2

Hypothetically Yours

What follows is a fable with a happy ending. It is my prediction that as we advance toward the close of this century, such tales will become less and less fabulous.

The radically decentralized corporation is a fundamentally different beast from the large conventional company. Let us start with the hypothetical Polaris Industries conglomerate. Founded back in the go-go era of the 1960s, Polaris had grown by the mid-1970s into a billion-dollar corporation. But in 1976, 1977, and 1978, its fortunes began to reverse. By 1979, red ink was beginning to appear on the books of some of its divisions. By 1980 it became clear to the board that unless drastic action was taken, the corporation would soon be in serious trouble. At this point, a nationally known management consultant was brought into the picture. His assignment: to study the organization's structure and policies, analyze the situation, and make recommendations with profit turnaround in mind.

The study took almost three months. The recommendations outlined in an 86-page consultant's report could be summarized in a single short sentence. *Decentralize radically; fire 80 percent of the headquarters staff and let your qualified division people do their own thing in their own way.*

The board decided to follow the consultant's recommendations. Polaris's president, some of his top aides, and several financial specialists and numbers men were fired. A new president, Bill Starbright, who had good experience as chief executive of a successful decentralized corporation, was hired. By

36

the end of the year, the transition from extreme centralization to radical decentralization was completed.

Manager's-Eye View of RD

If there is one man who fully understands and appreciates the transition from EC (Extreme Centralization) to RD, it is Harry Martin, formerly division manager and now president of Superior Folding Chair Co., acquired by Polaris back in 1968. Under EC, Harry functioned as a typical unit manager, responsible for the division's profit performance, but under the perpetual supervision and scrutiny of group vice president Roger Grouch and his numbers-oriented team. Harry still has occasional nightmares relating back to the Dark and Dismal Days, and so appreciates the Bright New World of the 1980s all the more.

It had taken some time for Martin to grow accustomed to the reality that he no longer had to check out every request with Grouch and clear with him before every major decision. He still exhibits the nervous habit of glancing back over his shoulder from time to time as a matter of course. He remembers, for example, the work done by his people on a capital request for new equipment to replace obsolete machinery, which, like Harry himself, was in momentary danger of breaking down.

He and his aides had worked many hours into several nights preparing a 100-page document in support of the request and had finally succeeded in winning approval, but only after nine revisions of the report and the resignation of one of his aides. Harry estimates that the delay in replacing the equipment cost the company more than $75,000.

RD put an end to Grouch and his cohorts and this kind of nonsense, for good, Harry hoped. Not a vindictive man, he wishes the former group vice president luck in finding a new job, preferably with one of Superior's major competitors.

Today Harry needs $6 million to build a new plant. Walking into the office of the corporate controller, he glances down at the slim briefcase in his hand and reflects on the difference between the Bright New World and the Dark Dismal Days. Back then, before RD, such a request would have required extensive and voluminous documentation. The proposal would have undergone line-by-line scrutiny, with Grouch and his hornrimmed MBAs probing every aspect of the budget in excruciating detail. Questions fired at him as if he were on the witness stand would have ranged far beyond such matters as anticipated return on investment and projected results. Grouch would have wanted a virtual guarantee from him that the new plant would pay off handsomely and, in so doing, would make a hero out of *him*.

Harry still winces, recalling the humiliation he had undergone while submitting to dehumanizing experiences of this kind. Typically, prior to the inquisition, he'd always had to put his busy staff to work compiling a great mass of detail. Then he would have to keep his cool through the inquisition itself, which almost invariably brought out the numbers boys' total lack of understanding of Superior's objectives and needs.

Following this ordeal he would have to return to the plant and await the Olympian decision. If it was "no," it meant he would be subjected to the added embarrassment of having to face his key people and confess that the project they had all worked so hard on had failed, a confession tantamount to his own failure as a manager.

Now under Starbright and decentralization, it was a whole different ball game, with his people the batters and pitchers, and himself the team's manager. Today, entering the financial executive's office, his briefcase contained a profit-and-loss statement, pertinent industry figures, and a sheet of financial support data. One of his top aides had worked up the information in a couple of days. He had reviewed and approved it.

His discussion with the controller, which took a half-hour or so, focused almost exclusively on money. It didn't attempt to dot all the i's or cross the t's. It was not a corporate exercise of purse-strings control as a means of imposing changes in policy. The controller's task was primarily that of a banker, which he was in effect. He rightfully needed to make sure this investment would be in the stockholders' interests. And that's *all* he needed to know. The whys, hows, and wherefores were none of his concern. He wasn't qualified to pass judgment on them, and he realized it. That was Harry's job, which is why they had made him president.

Under the new setup Harry was the number-one man at Superior. His people knew it. They knew it at headquarters.

And most important of all, *Harry* knew it. He respected himself and had the respect of his peers.

"A Good Man Is Hard to Find"

This has always been true, as the old jazz tune affirms, but under extreme centralization a good man may be not only hard to find but even harder to hire. How well Harry Martin could confirm this, remembering the old Dark and Dismal Days. Harry recalls the time he got the hottest of tips that "Chip" Callahan, ace sales manager for Foldamatic, Superior's toughest competitor, was having run-ins with his boss and was ripe for a change if approached tactfully, which, pragmatically interpreted, means being made an attractive offer. If there was one thing that could ensure Superior's vaulting ahead of Foldamatic, Harry knew, that thing was named "Chip" Callahan.

Proceeding gingerly but firmly, Harry made all the right moves and convinced Callahan he had a great present and even brighter future with Superior. The sales executive agreed to cross over. All that remained now was the purely routine task of getting headquarters approval. Bubbling with enthusiasm, for this was the chance of a lifetime. Harry paid a call on the corporation's executive vice president for marketing.

Like a schoolboy holding an all-A report card behind his back, Harry asked the vice president if he was ready to hear some good news.

"I'm always ready for good news" was the sober and cautious reply.

Harry proudly revealed their big break, gave a nutshell explanation of what it would mean in dollars and cents.

"Hmmmm. How much did you have to offer him?"

Harry named the figure. "It's high, but knowing Callahan, I can tell you it's the bargain of the century."

"Maybe so, but—"

The VP launched into a detailed lecture on the corporation's table of organization and what Callahan's salary would do to the rate structure. "I'll let you know what we decide."

The decision, unfavorable, took more than a week to reach Harry. Fuming, he went over Mr. Marketing's head and set up a meeting with the CEO. More time elapsed. He ultimately succeeded in showing the top man the light and getting his O.K. to close the deal. But by that time it was too late. "Chip" Callahan had made other arrangements.

Now under RD, things were different. Harry needed a bright, energetic merchandising director, and had just the right person to fill the job: Monica Maynard, now with Chaircroppers, Inc. The timing was perfect. Monica Maynard, he'd heard, was getting restless. He took her to lunch at the Savoy, turned on the charm and charisma, and hired her right on the spot. No need to check back with headquarters. No need to get the executive vice president of marketing's approval. In fact, that post no longer exists.

"I've Been Moved"—No More

A popular cliché in the data processing industry (which no longer applies) was the semibitter affirmation that IBM was simply an acronym for "I've been moved," so common at one time was the transfer of key employees from one facility of the electronics giant to another. Although the practice of shifting people from one location to another, whether they liked it or not, has declined in recent years, many highly centralized corporations still follow it as mindlessly and callously as ever. Polaris, in the old dismal days, was no exception.

Harry Martin still gets a queasy feeling in his gut reminiscing about the time the chess players at headquarters decided that Mike Cummings was just the man needed to take over an ailing plant in South Kalamazoo. The day Harry was *informed* of the decision, he all but split a corpuscle. Mike was the best manufacturing manager he'd ever had. They'd grown up together, helped build Superior together before the Polaris takeover in 1968. What's more, the Kalamazoo plant produced artificial flowers. Harry was damned if he could see the connection between folding chairs and artificial flowers.

But at one point, Harry recalled, he was assailed by feelings of guilt. What the hell! Maybe this was Mike's Big Chance. Who was he to stand in his way? The least he could do was present the proposition as objectively and unbiasedly as possible. Which he did.

"Are you kidding!" Mike exploded. "Transfer to Kalamazoo at this stage of my life! I'd have to be nuts."

40

Mike was a scoutmaster in town. He was president of the local trade association. His wife was into all kinds of local activities. His kids were on all kinds of teams and had close school ties. Mike wouldn't even give a second thought to the move.

The dire reaction from headquarters: "Harry, you know the policy here at Polaris—up or out. This is Cummings's big opportunity. I can't impress on you strongly enough . . ."

The story's punchline? You probably predicted it. Mike went to work for Foldamatic.

Today, automatic transfers of key people are no longer made as a matter of headquarters policy, because the corporation doesn't make such decisions. In the Dark and Dismal Days, Harry recalls, more than half of Polaris managers in the 25-to-40 age bracket had been moved at least three times over a ten-year period—within the United States and overseas. "During that period," he says, "the dropout rate was prodigious and Polaris managers were easy to pirate. Under radical decentralization, they are treated like people and turnover has dropped about 70 percent."

Today, Harry polls his key people to see how they feel about relocating. Their preferences are respected. If a manager wants to stay rooted, it isn't held against him, and it doesn't influence his career progress at home.

Superior Folding Chair has three different plants. On rare occasions transfer appears beneficial, but Harry is generally opposed to them as a matter of principle. He agrees with anthropologist Lionel Tiger's observation that moving people around deprives them of social continuity and stability and prevents them from becoming effective members of the community. Harry views the old policy as a kind of trafficking in human flesh. Sending in requisitions for people and having them filled like lunch orders may seem expedient and convenient at the time. But that's only one side of the picture. He remembers vividly the tough time he had and the hole that was created when Mike Cummings resigned rather than sitting still for the transfer imposed on him.

"The cost of training a replacement and the cost of the inefficiency that resulted for at least three to six months after his departure would be impossible to estimate," he says. "But if I had to hazard a guess, I'd say it was well into six figures. That would have occurred even if Mike had agreed to the transfer."

On the whole, he concludes, being human is profitable. And radical decentralization favors humanity.

Life Without Plato

One thing that impresses Harry any time he drops into headquarters for a chat with the controller or president is that the Giant Behemoth is gone. The behemoth—or Plato, as it was affectionately called by division executives for a while—was the huge powerful centralized computer installed by Polaris during the Dark and Dismal Days.

Unfortunately, the affection was shortlived. Plato lasted little more than two years and, featured in the consultant's evaluation report, helped pave the way to ultimate radical decentralization.

Plato was spawned on the heels of a bright remark by one of the ex-brains at corporate headquarters: "What we should do is get rid of all those little computers and get one big one, with all the divisions tying into it."

How can you argue with a brainstorm like that? Nobody did, especially since the idea was conceived by the ex-president's son-in-law Roger Grouch. Remember Roger? In any case, the recommendation had gone through like a knife through melting butter. The central computer had been installed at a prodigious cost and with the infusion of dozens of systems experts and programmers. Remote terminals were placed all over the units. Plato's awesome capacity, it was assumed, would be sufficient to meet every and any division need imaginable—and, as it turned out, every division whim as well.

You guessed the outcome. Within a year the central computer was swamped. Every division manager, it appeared, had come to the same conclusion. Now with Plato as close as the nearest terminal, there was no reason not to feed in all those tempting programs for which there never had seemed to be the time and money in the past.

Time-sharing quickly deteriorated into time-snaring. The divisional lineup to get on Plato was longer than the one for the 5:15 bus bound out of the city for suburbia. More corporate staff was recruited, but traffic bogged down nonetheless.

The tide couldn't be stemmed. Plato II, a fifth-generation machine, was installed, and being modular, the models kept coming. Headquarters began to look like the telephone company.

Profits multiplied faster than rabbits being fed aphrodisiacs—profits of the equipment suppliers and forms companies. Which brings to mind Levinson's Law of Information Explosion: "Paperwork expands to exceed the capacity of computers installed to create it."

At Superior Folding Chair's main plant, an extra wing was added to store all the new reports being generated. Naturally, all the information produced at the terminals—data about inventories, shipments, back orders, cash flow, salesmen's commissions, machine uptime and downtime, gross sales, net sales, key-account sales, purchases, accounts payable, accounts receivable, accounts unbelievable, you name it—had to be transmitted to headquarters as well, for here was the pulsating nerve center of the corporate enterprise.

In the old pre-Plato days, information was sparse and reliable. Now it was superabundant, and often manual duplication was needed, because you couldn't always depend on it.

Today, under RD, Plato is a relic in some used-equipment dealer's warehouse. A medium-size computer—cost-justified to the hilt—has been reinstalled at SFC. If a manager wants to know the number of folding chairs being sold to veterans' hospitals every month, broken down by territory and type of product, he's required to explain how this report will more than pay for itself. That extra wing at the main plant? A companywide cleanup was made after RD came in, and hundreds of bales of the reports there were sold off as scrap. The space is being used to store merchandise and components of the new product line Harry long had wanted to produce but, because of his failure to get Grouch's approval, had never gotten around to.

Businessman to Businessman

"How are the buffet tables going, Harry? Still feel the same way about them?"

Jim Frazier, Polaris's board chairman, and Harry were having a friendly casual conversation at headquarters one day.

"Well, Jim, the answers are, respectively, 'pretty good' and 'yes, definitely.' The line didn't take off quite as much like a thunderbolt as I had hoped. But it's gradually gaining dealer acceptance."

They were referring to the new line on which production had recently started. Harry had decided to diversify. Not Polaris. Harry.

"My feeling," he told Frazier, "and our market research confirms it, is that demand for these products is going to continue to build, maybe even exceed our original projections within five to ten years. There are no guarantees, of course, but that's the way I see it."

Frazier nodded, and they branched off to another topic.

Flying back home, Harry couldn't help but reflect how different the dialog would have been in the pre-RD days. It would have been another inquisition, with him on the witness stand again. Under Grouch, criteria had been set on an item-by-item basis for every product line made or sold by the subsidiaries—broken down to the nth degree in terms of market share, ROI, and a host of other factors as well. If a line failed to meet the criteria, regardless of how well it fit into the overall product mix or how significantly it helped fulfill customer needs, it was computer-zapped out of existence.

School Daze

One of the things Grouch and his goons liked to pitch in the Dark and Dismal Days before RD was the invaluable "services" corporate headquarters provided for all the divisions. One of the most priceless of these invaluable services was campus recruiting.

The way it worked, a team of corporate recruiters would show up at selected B schools toward the end of each semester, interview job candidates from the top 15 percent of the graduating class, pass out reams of recruitment literature, and hire the most promising seniors as management trainees. The recruits entered a year-long program, the centerpiece of which was rotation through Polaris's various divisions. After the program's completion, the current crop of trainees—those who survived the year's training—was more or less put up for grabs.

A three-day session was held with managers from each division in attendance. In a kind of reverse auction, managers made their bids for the candidates they felt, on the basis of insufficient evidence, were best. Where conflict was involved, the corporate human resources department, a spinoff of a spinoff of the personnel department, made the final allocation. For some time during this program Harry had thought it wasn't too bad a deal. In fact, one young man had turned out rather well despite the fact that he had graduated from Harvard. After all, Harry reasoned, along with other division managers, the corporation certainly had more clout on the campuses of such prestigious schools as Wharton, Stanford, Harvard, and Tuck than the divisions. Besides, as Grouch liked to point out, it's expensive to duplicate the recruitment process.

Now Harry realized he'd been brainwashed along with the others. For one thing, if you added up the cost of the corporate recruitment team, the mass of recruitment literature produced by outside public-relations firms, and the periodic meetings and seminars involved in the selection process, it would more than have paid for whatever duplication one could imagine. For another thing, although it was true that Polaris had more clout on campus than little old SFC, he eventually concluded that confining recruitment efforts to the prestige B schools—or to any B schools, for that matter—was limiting and restrictive.

With the advent of radical decentralization, recruitment rightfully reverted to the divisions. This served two purposes: it made the function a whole lot more flexible, and at the same time a lot more effective. One of the best sources Harry's personnel department was able to develop, for example, was large corporations that had not been decentralized and so were often bogged down by long and extensive training programs. A young woman hired six months ago who was turning into a star bluntly gave her main reason for quitting a big company while in the midst of a grueling training program to come to work for SFC: "After four years of high school and another four years of college, I've just about had it with long training programs. I want to get out in the field where the action is happening."

A universally held view among young people today. Also, under Polaris's program, a master's degree was mandatory. Harry's experience taught him that a master's degree does not a master make. He can now point to a couple of recently hired up-and-coming BBAs from state universities to prove his contention. A third revelation is that many bright young college graduates prefer going to work for small and medium-size companies. As one recruit put it: "You stand less danger of being lost in the shuffle."

Harry's final conclusion: under centralization, many of the corporate offerings touted as "services" actually turn out to be more *dis*services than anything else.

The Consulting Arm of Polaris

The pages of Manhattan's classified telephone directory list more than 600 consulting firms. This adds up to thousands of consultants. Nationwide, this figure can be multiplied several times. Management consulting is big business today, and there are times when even the most skilled executive can use the services of a well-qualified pro.

Although a competent enough president, Harry Martin is no exception. As he puts it, "You run into all kinds of problems in business, and an experienced consultant runs into all kinds of problems on a day-to-day basis. In fact, the name of his business is problems."

Harry remembers the time, pre-RD, when he was considering a marketing strategy he read about that had been applied successfully by operations in a different line of business. He was debating whether or not to propose it on an experimental basis to Roger Grouch and the corporate marketing department. But before doing so, and having Grouch pounce on him, he thought it might be a good idea to get a skilled consultant's views on the subject.

One day while at headquarters, he approached the head of the company's corporate consulting organization, presumably an independent body of experts. The top man was tied up in meetings all day, but an assistant asked Harry what he could do for him. The assistant nodded intelligently while Harry filled him in on the problem.

At the end he commented, "It's a problem."

"What do you think I should do about it? What would you do in my position?"

The assistant nodded some more. "It certainly warrants some study. I'll put the engagement on my list."

"What list?"

"My list of consulting engagements."

It turned out the consulting arm, backlogged for more than six months, was in something of a sling. Harry eventually did get a response. But by that time he had forgotten what the original idea was all about.

Polaris still has a consulting group, but the whole concept has changed. In the Dark and Dismal Days, the divisions were captive "clients." This accounted for the six-month backlog of "engagements." From the divisions' point of view, most of the engagements weren't very engaging. Consulting systems specialists would descend on the units from time to time as the spirit—or the Roger Grouches—dictated. They made studies, and cranked out recommendations. If a division manager didn't like a particular recommendation, he was required to produce figures to prove why it wasn't beneficial. Where there was more than numbers involved, as is often the case, the recommendation was imposed, like it or not.

Under the new RD structure, the corporate consulting group is required to *sell* its services to the divisions. At the division's election, the unit might avail itself of the service at a very reasonable cost, turn to an outside consultant for help, or use no consultant at all.

At the moment a consultant from corporate headquarters is in Harry's spacious office with the gilt letters HARRY MARTIN, president, neatly stenciled on the door. In an animated discussion with Harry and his controller, he is giving his views regarding the direction SFC should take in streamlining its EDP, accounting, and production-control functions. Running through Harry's mind are the pros and cons of taking advantage of corporate consulting services as opposed to bringing in Booz-Allen or Cresap-McCormick.

A good feeling, Harry mused. As decision maker, it's nice to know you have the power to make the decisions. This wasn't always the case.

No More Labor Pains

The marital dealings between labor and management can never be free of aggravation and grief. But now, under RD, the situation is at least livable. In some respects corporation-

47

wide bargaining is built into many of the nation's labor contracts, so that, even under decentralization, Polaris exercises a general umbrella involvement. And, if Harry is of a mind to, he can consult with the corporation's labor expert.

But the situation is in no way as it used to be. Harry is SFC's president. He acts like the president. He is treated like the president. And the division's labor attorney answers only to him. In short, wherever the shots are callable, Harry calls them. Most significant, when problems erupt and when negotiations are under way, he deals personally and directly with the union. So far as they are concerned, *he,* not some horn-rimmed guy the corporation whisked out for the purpose, is SFC.

Take the time they got into a hassle over work standards for the new buffet-table line. Harry, his plant manager, and his labor guy had sat down in the small conference room with the plant steward and two guys from union headquarters. It had been hot and heavy going for a while, but they had hammered out an agreement with a little human give here and a little human give there. In the end they'd shaken hands and were buddies again. The key: mutual respect and good faith, by-products Old Hornrim had never been able to achieve.

Harry could also tell you about the advantages of having a local lawyer on hand during certain negotiations, as opposed to the corporate specialists. His guy knows the company and work situation intimately. He understands the problems and personalities involved. He's realistic, down to earth. The headquarters guys tended to think in terms of big numbers, big issues. The small problems seemed to annoy them, as if they were beneath their station and dignity. But Harry, a hard-headed businessman who's been around a long time, could tell you that most big problems are nothing more than a collection of small ones.

Another thing, the guys from Corporate were in the habit of thinking in terms of Polaris's 55,000 employees. They couldn't be bothered with issues involving just a few hundred. A typical reaction: "Give them what they want; it's not worth arguing over." But concessions here lead to concessions there, and it can get to be a habit. Harry was happy those days were done with.

Another RD blessing involved benefits. When Polaris was

centralized, benefit plans were all formulated on the 73rd floor. And many of the benefits Harry inherited were anything but beneficial so far as he was concerned, and in some cases the rank-and-filers as well. After all, who knows better what the local people want and need than the managers on the scene?

Today there's a mixed bag of benefits. Some of the work done by Corporate isn't undoable. And in some cases options exist. But when a benefits hassle crops up, it's Harry and his benefits man who sit down with the union representatives, not a guy from 2,000 miles away. And if Harry gets the notion that, "Hey, I think what my people really want and need is a dental plan. It might be a highly effective motivator," he has the power and authority to follow through on his idea if he wishes to. On health, Harry's people chose to contract with a new HMO in the area. After reviewing their proposal, Harry said, "Sure, go ahead."

It's a great feeling to be able to say, "Sure, go ahead." Makes you feel like you're running the show.

Oh, Yes, the Game Has a Name

Polaris Industries, Inc., just in case you got a false idea, isn't a charitable institution. Nor is it an experimental research laboratory where managers are given the leeway to play wild and far-out games. Polaris is a profits-geared organization. If the game has a name, that name is RESULTS. So long as Harry produces results that keep the stockholders happy, the show is all his to run.

But as we said, the guy is an absolute realist. As Harry puts it himself, "Suppose I decide I don't want to make folding chairs any more? Suppose I get the notion to make Frisbees, or publish a magazine, or move the business to Vegas and turn it into a gambling casino or a legalized brothel?"

Ho, ho, ho! At this point Junior gets a spanking and Big Daddy takes over. Under Polaris's new RD setup, division presidents get a free hand. But the arm doesn't go along with it. They must operate within reason. If Polaris buys a successful chair company, that's what it wants: a successful chair company. Harry can go into folding tables if he wants, maybe even folding stepladders. But Polaris's chief interest is folding money. If the receipt of that seems to be in jeopardy, old Harry's in trouble. He can diversify if he thinks it makes sense within the context of his operation. But he can't go off on fruitcake ventures that might make the folding-chair business fold.

Needless to say, that doesn't bother Harry a whit. He's a practical and level-headed chief executive with both feet planted firmly on his desk. That's where he'd like to keep them, and under RD the prospects look more promising every day.

PART II

Why Radical Decentralization?

CHAPTER 3

The Lack of Autonomy

In 1776, coincident with America's independence, the Scottish economist Adam Smith revealed in his just-published *The Wealth of Nations* his dream of the great "invisible hand." The dream in a nutshell: that each individual, working on his own behalf for his personal aggrandizement, creates in the process a society that is best not only for the individual but for the nation as a whole. This entrepreneurial spirit boosts the standards not only of the host nation but of other nations as well.

As any student of history would confirm, there were flagrant excesses and abuses involved in the entrepreneurial foment of the nineteenth and early twentieth centuries in this country. But out of the foment emerged progress and growth. Commenting on this phenomenon, Theodore J. Gordon, President of The Futures Group, states:

> The complex mesh of forces that led to these huge changes was driven not by fiat and design, but largely by individual innovators, entrepreneurs, and social revisionists. The names that come immediately to mind are Edison, Ford, Armour, Birdseye, Pullman, McCormick, Whitney, Hartford, Singer, Howe, Rockefeller, and Morgan: organizers, entrepreneurs, go-getters carrying ideas and concepts to the market, creating markets. Theirs is the history of enterprise.*

* "The Revival of Enterprise," Mitchell Prize Award Paper for the Third Biennial Conference on Growth Policy, October 28–31, 1979, p. 6.

Death of the Entrepreneur

Despite the excesses—most of which would not be possible today—it was the entrepreneurial spirit which, in large measure, made America great. And sadly, it is the decline of this spirit, the bureaucratic defusing of it, which contributes strongly toward the nation's falling back from world leadership in recent years.

We needn't look far for the proof. In 1980, for the first time in history, the United States rated number two in the production and sale of automobiles, with more Japanese than American cars introduced in the world marketplace. According to a recent *Business Week* report:

> In the 1970s the U.S. lost 23 percent of its share of the world market, compared with a 16 percent decline during the 1960s. U.S. manufacturers' share of the domestic market also fell more in the most recent decade than earlier. The losses in the 1970s are particularly telling, because they came in the wake of a 40 percent depreciation in the value of the dollar, which made U.S. exports cheaper and foreign imports more expensive. The decline in the U.S. position in the 1970s alone amounted to some $125 billion in lost production and a loss of at least 2 million industrial jobs.*

Among the hardest-hit industries, apart from the automobile industry, are agricultural, textile, and metalworking machinery, machine tools, pharmaceuticals, organic chemicals, and consumer electronics, to mention a few.

We would do well, I think, to take a cue from the Russians. Despite its vast power and natural resources, the Soviet Union appears unable to meet the daily needs of its people. Though the typical Russian citizen is better off today than in the time of the czar, quality goods are rare and expensive, gloom and disgruntlement widespread.

As *Time* notes:

> The main reason is a system that will not, and perhaps cannot, work. The Soviet economy has always been stultified by too much central planning, too little entrepreneurial incentive. Factories, farms, and individual workers are caught up in a machine that spews forth quotas and directives, sucks up output, inefficiently manufactures and distributes goods, and

* June 30, 1980.

rarely rewards initiative. Those deficiencies, inefficiencies, and inflexibilities are now catching up with the economy and slowing it down. During the 1980s, Western experts predict, the Soviet growth rate will drop even lower than last year's [1979's] estimated 0.7 percent.*

It's ironic that here we are, two nations diametrically opposed in terms of philosophy of government and lifestyle, yet both America and the Soviet Union seem to be reeling under the same stifling and crippling economic disease. Our only bright glowing hope is that a *free* economy at least has the flexibility needed to change and improve. The question is: will we respond to the challenge?

WHATEVER HAPPENED TO CHARLEY?

Remember old Charley? A true manager, he used to run the plant. The buck stopped at his desk. Smart chief executive. Gutsy. His instincts based on savvy, field-based education, and years of experience, worked most of the time. Built the company from a six-man operation to a $30-million-a-year enterprise. But you don't hear much about him any more. He's been largely replaced by a Sure-Thing-Profits-Now management system that uses charts, matrixes, and computer printouts to plot the maybe element out of the business.

Too bad about Charley. He doesn't have much to say anymore about running the business. But if you happen to run into him, you'll find he likes to talk about his heritage, other "old-fashioned" managers whose philosophy was similar to his: "You do the best you can on the basis of whatever facts and know-how you can gather. But what the hell, to a degree business, like life, is a gamble. You have to toss the dice on occasion."

If you have the time to chat with Charley, he might tell you the story about an old buddy of his, Heublein's Rudolf Kunett, and the time he had a warehouse filled with vodka that no one wanted to buy. It happened that at the same time a restaurateur friend, Jack Morgan, was stuck with a lot of ginger beer that was selling about as well as the vodka. And Morgan had a pal who made copper mugs that weren't moving at all. So the three put their heads together and came up

* Special issue on the Soviet Union, June 23, 1980.

with the "Moscow Mule," which was vodka and ginger beer served in a copper mug. You probably guessed the result: sales started to rocket.

In the old days there was no shortage of gutsy manager types like Rudolf Kunett and Charley. Charley could reel them off on his fingertips.

Like Marcellus Fleming Berry of American Express, who dreamed up the first "traveler's check."

Or Willis Haviland Carrier, who developed the first air-conditioning system.

Or Dr. Edwin Land, whose Polaroid camera presents you with a picture within a minute after it is snapped.

Or Orville S. Caesar, the Greyhound chief executive who introduced the first dual-level touring bus.

The list of America's imaginative and courageous entrepreneurs could go on at some length. But the list of those spawned in recent years isn't nearly so great. The reason isn't difficult to pinpoint. Could you imagine such offbeat innovations as the traveler's check, the air conditioner, or the dual-level bus being developed if Berry, Carrier, or Caesar had to wade through layers of numbers-oriented, profits-now, remote-control managers at corporate headquarters for approval? No way! It would have involved taking a chance.

One major cause of Charley's demise is "the system." Big business, which appears to be swallowing up more and more of little business, is for the most part decision-activated by the numbers. Wall Street is largely to blame, because when the stock analyst probes, he's more interested in the figures than he is in management structure, capability, and experience, or the long-run ability of the managers.

Another culprit that helped do Charley in is the modern "instant gratification" mentality. Profits now, and let the long range take care of itself. Young business-school computer-geared finanthropologists are quick to take the cue from their fast-buck superiors, so they are now layered in solidly in the centralized corporations, leaving little room for the maverick. If you want to climb, you conform.

A *Business Week* Special Report sums it up neatly:

> . . . for the most part, today's corporate leaders are "professional managers"—business mercenaries who ply their skills

for a salary bonus but rarely for a vision. And those skills are generally narrow and specialized. Just as the general practitioner who made house calls is a dim memory, so is the hands-on corporate leader who rose through the ranks, learning every aspect of the business before managing it. Today's managers are known as great marketers, savvy lawyers, or hard-nosed financial men. Lacking a gut feeling for the *gestalt* of their businesses, they see managing by the numbers as their only recourse.*

The report further notes a recent study of 50 companies by the West Coast consulting firm of Theodore Barry & Associates. One conclusion of this survey was that "most executives have never participated in the line-management process, so there is no sensitivity to the problems in this area." My personal experience confirms this finding. Too often in large centralized organizations, top-management interest and attention don't extend beyond financial reports. Ample lip service is given to the importance of innovation and initiative, but the managers who win the promotions and bonuses are the ones who juggle the numbers most successfully.

A classic example of the modern numbers fixation is the publishing industry. Dozens of independent publishers, some of them American institutions, have been gobbled up in recent years by supercentralized conglomerates. An editor friend told me recently, "All the old joy and excitement have been taken out of the job. An editor knows no greater thrill than discovering a bright new talent, helping to develop and hone a rough stone of a book with powerful thoughts and emotions obscured and hidden into a polished giant of a gem. But intuition and experience don't count for much anymore. Today, a computer printout tells you whether or not a submitted manuscript is worth processing. The editor isn't even consulted. If it looks like a sure thing, the decision is go. Experimentation in art and departure from the norm are out."

What the numerologists don't seem to realize is that you can't program management savvy and experience into a computer. You can't plot hands-on judgment and instinct on a decision grid. One of the dilemmas you frequently encounter as an on-the-scene manager involves this matter of priorities. Where do you spend your time: on money-making opportu-

*June 30, 1980.

57

nities, or the business problems and bottlenecks you keep running into? Devote time to the problems and you may bypass the opportunities. Concentrate on the opportunities and the problems may get worse.

I have no way of determining this, of course, but I've wondered at times what the outcome of that bungled and aborted attempt to rescue the Iranian hostages might have been had the skilled and experienced "managers" on the scene been permitted to decide whether to go or to pull back. Those men were trained and determined. They knew what to do and how to do it. Was the brain trust in Washington thousands of miles away better equipped to decide, using war maps, charts, and probability statistics? Perhaps it was. But I wouldn't want to bet on it.

A ROSE BY ANY OTHER NAME

A rose by any other name might—and very often does—smell sweeter, at least to the cultivators of the rose. As a vice president of American Standard, Inc., following its acquisition of my medium-size family-owned company, I was often asked: "Doesn't the name American Standard enhance the image of a company like Steelcraft Manufacturing?"

Maybe it does in a way. But again, when you ponder a question like this, you have to realize that entrepreneurial pride and human nature are key factors. When WABCO became part of American Standard, it didn't want to be known as an American Standard company. It was WABCO, and proud of it. Same thing for Mosler Safe. And the same thing for Steelcraft. I was duly impressed by American Standard's name and reputation in industry. But Steelcraft was the organization I had poured my life's blood into. I had seen it develop from a small fledgling enterprise into a substantial one. I had lived through its hardships and turmoil. I had shared in its achievements and triumphs.

Identity and recognition constitute an important part of the entreprenurial makeup. No matter how big or important or impressive Daddy might be, Junior needs his own voice, his own face, his own name. There are individual situations where the acquired company isn't as well established in the industry as it would like to be, and in such cases being identified with the large parent company undoubtedly does add some stature.

But even where being associated with the big powerful parent has a clear advantage, human feelings get in the way.

I don't care who it is—if it's Suzy Belle Ice Cream acquired by Borden's, or Mineola Carpet Tack acquired by U.S. Steel, or Pomona Envelope Co. acquired by Xerox—the organization's principals are usually as proud of their individual corporate names as they are of their personal names. Acquired by American Standard, I could never forget that in my heart and soul Bob Levinson was Steelcraft, and that a little piece of me will always be Steelcraft.

THAT ALL-IMPORTANT PERSONAL STAKE

The motivational impact of emotional involvement in the enterprise, that critically important personal stake that includes but also extends beyond compensation, is all too often disregarded or inadequately understood by the remote-control executive on the 73rd floor.

Typically, the management team of the highly centralized corporation thinks of divisional executives as well as performance results in terms of numbers. It manipulates managers by wire-transmitted management mandate, much as a child manipulates his collection of tin soldiers. The head man or woman on the scene sees John as ambitious, Sam as mildly frustrated, Max as potential talent waiting to be developed, Mary as a bright and sensitive woman who longs for independence and status—human beings with human needs, wants, and weaknesses. And on the basis of these human qualities he makes assignments, provides coaching, grants personal recognition and rewards as required, responds to human strengths and shortcomings with individual and organizational objectives in mind. Whereas the corporation dehumanizes the operation through depersonalized planning and action, the sensitive executive on the scene customizes his planning and action with people in view.

A weighty consideration the independent entrepreneur must live with day in and day out involves that daily bank balance. How much money do I have to work with? Can I pay all those bills and still meet the payroll? What percentage of my receivables can I count on getting by the end of the week? Will Davis leave if I don't give him a raise? Can I afford to shell out the money he wants? What will it do to the organizational structure? How much can I put into public relations? into advertising?

When you never see a check come in and never have to sign a check yourself, a whole different mentality and frame of reference are involved. You don't think like a businessman. Your thinking is depersonalized, just like the computer printouts you count on to guide your decision making and planning. You lose sight of the individual and his stake in the enterprise.

When I was at American Standard, I conducted a little experiment. I was responsible for the Building Specialties Group, and we took reps from each of three product divisions—fireplaces, doors, and movable walls—and set up a training program to familiarize each salesperson with all three products. Then we sent them out into the field with instructions to sell the three product lines.

I wasn't surprised by the outcome. Each rep from each division of the company sold his own product, seriously shortchanging the other two. On a remote basis, working from headquarters, I couldn't get them involved. They went through the motions, but the spirit was missing. They identified with their own product line. It's where their personal stake and feeling was rooted.

Another time we had a distributor in Hawaii, a good-size company with a catalog a foot high. This outfit handled a wide variety of products. If someone wanted a flagpole, they'd get a line of flagpoles and put it into the catalog. They'd do the same thing if someone asked for mousetraps or door chimes. When we tried to get them to sell our doors, they said sure, and into their catalog they went. That's about the only movement the doors saw, into the catalog. They certainly didn't move in the field.

WHY ENTREPRENEURS SELL OUT

Since it is so frustrating and dehumanizing for an executive, particularly one who is accustomed to being his company's chief decision maker for years, suddenly to find himself in a position where he is little more than a glorified policeman or order taker, one might wonder why so many ex-top executives find themselves in this spot. Why do so many former owners and principals dive mindlessly into the pool without checking first if it contains any water? Why do businessmen sell their businesses, some of them built and developed over many years in the face of unimaginable hardship and sacrifices? If anyone should have the answer to these questions it is I, Cockeyed Plunger number one.

Steelcraft Manufacturing Co. had its ups and downs, its triumphs and reverses, as occurs in every business. But by and large we were a successful, consistently profitable and, if I say so myself, intelligently managed organization that had grown in a couple of decades from a tiny ten-employee nonentity in the industry to one of its best-known and most highly respected companies with a reputation for top-quality products. How did I feel about Steelcraft? When I walked through one of its doors in a big-city skyscraper, it gave me a thrill that would be hard to describe. I felt a sensation of power and status, which I must confess at times went to my head. It gave me a very special satisfaction to know how many fine men and women relied on the company for their livelihoods and how many had risen to important positions of trust and expertise under my tutelage. Steelcraft? In a nutshell, I loved it.

Why then did we sell? Why have so many others in a similar situation sold out to conglomerates? Why is the sellout continuing, why are more and more cockeyed plungers taking the big dive each year? The reasons are simple.

Certainly a major cause of the sellout is the body of tax law in this country, which, had it been specially designed with the undermining of entrepreneurship in mind, couldn't have achieved this goal more effectvely. There are any number of strong and valid motivations that drive businesspeople to found and operate enterprises of their own. And whatever the rewards, surely one prize must be the accumulation of capital and the perquisites money can buy. Yet there is no way that the entrepreneur who owns his own business can accumulate significant capital in America, except at his death, and even then it is taxed to the hilt.

The body of tax law is only one major vise that is squeezing the small entrepreneur to death in America. There's another, in many industries equally deadly. It is called regulation—literally millions of rules that hogtie thousands of small-company owners, driving many into bankruptcy and beyond. It has been estimated that the cost of commerce and industry to comply with the soaring mountains of regulatory demands will exceed $120 billion this year. A boon to the paper industry, government regulation is forcing increasing numbers of small entrepreneurs out of the marketplace.

The large corporation, for all its inefficiency, is better positioned to cope with both regulation and the tax laws. It has batteries of specially trained staffers to pinpoint the loopholes and fill out the endless reports. What's more, the large corporation has the know-how and connections to "manipulate the levers of power," get special favors, as former Secretary of the Treasury William E. Simon states the case, to influence the rules and lawmakers. Big-company lobbyists are active on the political scene. With high stakes in bureaucratic decisions, they monitor proposed legislation, dole their dollars strategically, make their presence and preferences felt.

"Put all these factors together," says Simon, "and you have a perfect formula for victimizing little guys, enhancing the power of the big operators, and achieving economic effects that are the opposite of what we have been promised."*

All of which eventually leads more and more harassed businesspeople to throw in the sponge and say, "The hell with it! The game is no longer worth the prize." So, when the conglomerator knocks, they respond.

The Deciding Factor

For as far as the eye can see, the corporate graveyard is strewn with the corpses of managers who died because they made weak-kneed decisions or couldn't move quickly enough when decisions were needed.

According to an old Chinese proverb, "A wise man makes his own decisions, an ignorant man follows public opinion." Modern, "sophisticated" corporations do neither. They follow a course all their own. They program computers to work up the decisions, using an intricate network of internal checks and balances to guarantee accuracy. As a result, the arithmetic is almost always right. The only thing flawed is the judgment. Because however brilliant the science and technology, man has

*"Speaking Out," *Inc.,* January 1981, p. 18.

yet to invent a machine that can successfully substitute numbers juggling for human experience.

Worse yet, computers don't even *make* the decisions; they merely *set up* the decisions so that, in the centralized organization, remote-control managers can give the go or no-go command. Too often, as my sad experience trying to function effectively in a centralized environment proved time and again, the action is too little too late. The result is that programs are bogged down and delayed, opportunities slip by unapproached, managerial enthusiasm fades and dies. Corporate wheels grind sluggishly, and investment analysts begin to take potshots.

Massachusetts management consultant Charles H. Ford states the case succinctly enough:

> Strange, isn't it, that corporate tempo, the one factor that probably contributes most to corporate success (or lack of it), is the one most ignored.
>
> The tempo of a company—the speed with which it moves, makes and implements decisions, identifies and solves problems, grasps opportunities, reacts to competitive pressures, or adapts to abrupt changes in marketing patterns and business climates—is something to which most executives and corporate bodies remain blissfully indifferent.
>
> Yet, this is understandable. In this age of the computer, we like to deal with things that can be precisely measured. Obviously, tempo cannot be.*

SOME FAVORITE WAYS TO AVOID DECISIONS

Centralized Hookmanship. The surest way for a centralized company to trigger decision paralysis is to turn over the decision-making task to a centralized group. In fact, annihilation by committee is practiced so often one would think it's a prime objective of centralized corporations.

A study was conducted a couple of decades ago at the University of Michigan in an effort to measure individual against team performance. Participants were divided into two groups with comparable skills, education, and intelligence. Each person in the first group was given certain tasks to perform indi-

* Nation's Business, June 1973.

vidually. Members of the other group were given the same tasks to perform as a team.

The experiment's most significant conclusion was that the tendency to conform nearly doubles when people work at a group task, as opposed to an individual endeavor. Not only that, it usually takes a committee at least twice as long to come up with the answer.

Centralized hookmanship is the art of getting off the decision-making hook by getting others involved in the decision-making process. This technique comes in handy at times, and managers with experience in centralized companies have the finest training ground in the world.

A product-development executive I know in the cosmetics industry was being pressed by his boss, the president of the company, to evaluate a recently introduced competitive product to determine if they should come out with a similar product. The product man felt this decision would be premature, that they should let a waiting period of six months to a year go by before gauging the item's market potential. This would allow time to investigate and analyze customer response.

When he expressed this view to the president, the chief executive refused to go along with it. "I don't want to take any chances on missing the boat. Get on it as soon as you can."

My friend was convinced he was right and his boss was wrong. But he couldn't ignore a direct order from the chief. So he shrewdly appointed a committee of three aides and turned over the assignment to them.

A week or so later, when the president asked how the evaluation was coming along, he replied, "I've got a group working on it now."

This satisfied the boss, and the product man as well. There was no way, he knew, that the group would be forthcoming with a decision before six months at least.

For want of a signature. Another centralized decision crippler is the authorization mishmash a manager often has to wade through in a bureaucratic environment to get something done. A division executive I know recently told me of a rare opportunity that arose to buy a bankrupt company's stock and equipment at a cost that was approximately 50 percent of the market price. The deal, if consummated, would have resulted in a cost avoidance, or profit gain, in excess of $250,000. But since the transaction would have required an expenditure of over $5,000, the group vice president's O.K. was needed. Without his signature, the check couldn't be issued.

My friend called New York at once and was told the vice president was in Europe on a business trip. It took a glib and desperate soliloquy to convince his assistant of the deal's importance, and of the urgency of contacting his boss as soon as humanly possible. The assistant eventually, and reluctantly, promised to do what he could. What he could do wasn't good enough. It took him two days to get in touch with his boss. By that time a competitor had snatched up the bargain stock and equipment.

The study: A study in centralized bungling. Still another popular ploy designed to stifle a decision is to watch it die on the vine. I know of few responses more frustrating to a division manager with a pressing problem or hot opportunity in need of a quick decision than his boss's promise to "study the situation," or "take the matter under advisement." In effect, this is often a decision not to decide. If I had a dollar for every decision turned over to a "task force" for study or to a consultant for investigation and evaluation, I would be a very wealthy man today. In fact, a consultant friend admitted to me that more than half the studies conducted by his firm either should have been done by the client or shouldn't have been done to begin with.

THE INJUSTICE OF JUSTIFICATION

Justification in the centralized corporation is a two-edged sword, and I can tell you from experience that both edges are dull.

Edge number one involves the deadening, time-consuming, and humiliating process a division manager must go through in justifying capital expenditures before getting them approved. An astute manufacturing executive I know recently decided to tool up in anticipation of launching a new product line. Enthusiasm for the projected introduction ran high throughout the division since exciting innovations were involved. Here, division management decided, was its chance to get a big jump on major competitors.

The manufacturing executive knew exactly what had to be done in terms of construction, personnel, and the purchase of new equipment and materials. Three quarters of a million dollars was needed to bring the plan to fruition. The timing was tight, but all systems were go. The only thing still needed was headquarters approval. The manufacturing executive and his boss, the division manager, flew into New York, hoping to quickly tie a knot on the package, get back home, and start moving.

They found to their dismay no less than 11 corporate experts waiting for them when they arrived at headquarters. "It's your baby," the division manager told the manufacturing man. "Take the floor."

The executive made a brief but eloquent and quite effective presentation, which included all major highlights of the new-product launching plan. The team of 11 listened in silence. But when the presentation was over, a frontal attack was made that would have done Knute Rockne proud.

"Why will you need three automatic screw machines?" a line backer wanted to know.

"How can you be assured of product acceptance?" the quarterback asked.

"Why are two foremen required?"

"How many suppliers did you contact before deciding on Acme?"

And so on, and so forth.

In the end, approval was ultimately obtained. But only after a three-week delay and a rash of picayune alterations. By that time the schedule was shot and division enthusiasm for the project substantially diminished.

Edge number two involves justification from the other side of the fence and, in large measure, explains edge number one. To prove he is brilliant, perceptive, frugal, knowledgeable, and deeply concerned about corporate profits, each headquarters expert has to throw his six cents into the pot. Here he is earning—or, correction, *getting*—$39,500 a year plus fringes for giving the corporation the benefit of his six years at Harvard and his acquired expertise, and he is damned well certain to hold on to what he's got with bulldog determination and grit. He's got a secretary, a car, an apartment, and a key to the private john, and he's going to knock himself out to justify his job. He may be a corporate purchasing manager, and even if he never bought a thing in his life, he's going to make it his business to know why three screw machines, four batches of steel, and 33 overhead fluorescent lights are required.

So you can see why centralized corporate justification usually adds up to about 98 percent meddlesome nonsense and 2 percent justice—a devastating mixture that quickly extinguishes any remaining entrepreneurial spirit in the company.

STRIPPING MANAGERS OF THEIR SELF-WORTH

As far back as the seventeenth century, the French philosopher François de la Rochefoucauld recognized the important role a strong sense of self-worth plays in the fortunes of men and women. In *Maxims* (1665) he wrote:

> There is a kind of greatness which does not depend upon fortune; it is a certain manner that distinguishes us, and which seems to destine us for great things; it is the value we insensibly set upon ourselves; it is by this quality that we gain the reverence of other men, and it is this which commonly raises us more above them than birth, rank, or even merit itself.

When a presumed leader or executive is told what to do when it's his rightful job to make the decision, or when a task that is properly his is done for him by proxy, the effect—apart from a probable bungling of the job—is to undermine his self-worth.

A classic example comes to mind. In the cosmetics industry a not uncommon arrangement is for the supplier to work with key customers on an ad hoc basis on a cooperative or shared-cost advertising program. Under this setup the customer places product ads in local newspapers, and if the supplier agrees there's a good chance the pull will more than make up the expense, the supplier contracts to pay half the cost.

The general manager of a small-to-medium-size company, acquired by a large pharmaceutical corporation, was approached by his advertising manager and asked to approve such an arrangement with one of the company's important accounts. He reviewed the figures and the results of similar arrangements made in the past, estimated the potential, and gave his approval. The customer was notified, and a program extending over two holiday promotional periods was agreed upon. Since the acquisition, however, it was mandatory that all expenditures exceeding a rather nominal sum be sent to headquarters for final approval. This was done as a matter of course.

You guessed the result. The numbers man in Suite 7304 plotted a few angles on his grid, consulted the latest computer printout, referred to a critical-path diagram, and sent back the cooperative advertising requisition marked DISAPPROVED. The irate general manager got on the phone.

"Oh damn!" he protested, "this has been standard operating procedure for years. I reviewed that requisition myself."

"Sorry. According to the most current marketing forecast for that part of the country—"

The general manager hung up. Red-faced, he broke the bad news to the customer, who hung up on *him* and withdrew the account. What this harebrained proxy action did to the executive's feeling of self-worth and the self-esteem of his advertising manager isn't difficult to guess. Fortunately, the general manager had the good sense to resign after landing a high-paying job with a leading competitor.

Kurt R. Student, a psychologist and partner in the management consulting firm of Dallis, De Young, and Student, of Grand Rapids, Michigan, defines the four major leadership factors. Number one on his list is *support:* behavior that enhances someone else's feeling of personal worth and importance. Even if the numbers man at headquarters had been correct in his computer-based judgment that the proposed shared advertising constituted a dubiously profitable venture—a judgment I wouldn't want to bet on—the undermining effect of his mindless action certainly was more detrimental to the company's profit objectives than any small loss might have been.

HOW TO PINPOINT THE CON ARTISTS

Feigning decentralization pays off for the centralized companies. In recruiting executives and acquiring companies especially, you can score brownie points by convincing managers you're wooing that you're all gung ho for freedom of decision making and the entrepreneurial spirit. I think I can safely say that if 10 percent of the corporations that claim to be radically decentralized actually *were* radically decentralized, the economy would be in much better shape.

In my experience I find that evaluating a company's decision-making ability is a good way to determine if it is truly decentralized or merely paying lip service to the concept. To arrive at this determination, I usually ask the following questions:

- With one or more specific decisions in mind, how long did it take the company to make the decision?
- How many managers are usually involved when a decision is made? Is it made by one key executive or more often by a committee?
- Are a significant number of actions that should have been taken not taken because it took too long to decide?
- When decisions are permitted to drag, what is usually the reason?
- Where delays occur, who is usually responsible?
- Was the time lag caused by poor coordination on the part of various individuals or departments involved?
- Was the delay a result of characteristically slow corporate tempo, tail dragging being the norm?
- Could the delay be attributed to one or more managers being afraid to rock the boat or make a personal commitment?

Admittedly, such answers aren't easy to come by if you're an outsider. But where they are available, they're usually a pretty good tipoff to whether or not the organization is effectively decentralized. Typically, in the bureaucratic centralized company, key decisions take too long to come by; too many people are brought into the act; corporate tempo is slow, with opportunities flushed down the drain as a result; and managers are characteristically afraid to speak up for what they believe in.

DECISION PARALYSIS AS A PRIME DISENCHANTMENT FACTOR

There's another aspect to inflexibility, or bogged-down decision making, that escapes the eye and mind of many a manager. An executive recruiter I know summed it up with a chuckle. "It's good for business."

His business.

"Did you know," he told me, "that one of the chief reasons many talented managers decide to make a change is inflexibility in the top-executive suite?"

He reeled off a list of executives from large U.S. corporations, many of whom you would recognize, who quit high-level jobs in response to pirating by competitors or offers from other companies, because they were unable to get top managers or the board of directors to move off the dime.

It is terribly frustrating to an ambitious and talented executive to see his programs and goals stymied because they're snarled up in an endless progression of meetings, or put in limbo by a task force whose continuing "investigation" serves to stall a decision. Thus, as my experience has taught me, decision paralysis causes the typical centralized company to lose out, not only in the marketplace, but among key employees as well.

I know a gifted research director who was fired following a dispute with his boss. Urgently in need of a job, he was approached by a recruiter who told him "a large and prestigious company" was critically in need of his specialized experience and, having considered his background and qualifications, was "very favorably impressed."

"We'll have to go through the formality of interviews with the president and all that," he told the scientist, "but the way I read it, your employment is a virtual shoo-in, and at a higher price than what you were getting."

The research director was more than mildly interested until he heard the name of the company. At this point his polite response was, thanks but no thanks. The company's reputation for inflexibility had spread throughout the industry. The scientist knew the research director he would have replaced, a man who was resigning because getting approval for a major project or program was tantamount to moving a recalcitrant elephant.

Important as compensation is, it has been my experience that many managers would prefer the kind of job where they were given more independence and authority and less pay to one where they received higher pay but would have to go through agonizing and humiliating throes to get a go-ahead decision from top management.

Where self-esteem is concerned, impressive-sounding titles help, and so do impressive salaries and perquisites. But what helps most is the feeling and pride of achievement, of *doing it on your own,* of leading others and being the boss. In most centralized corporations I have seen, division managers are made to know in a dozen embarrassing ways who the boss really is. It frustrates not only achievement but one's individual feeling of self as well. In the decentralized operation you're *someone*, part of a winning combination. In the centralized company, more often than not you're a secondary title and number, and your nose is rubbed in this reality every day of the week.

CHAPTER 4

The Human Factor

"Habit is a cable," Horace Mann once wrote. "We weave a thread of it every day until it becomes so strong we cannot break it."

Centralization, through its bigness, standardization, and computerized decision making, fosters habitual behavior. Rules and strictures become organizational entrenchments. Even if individuals want to build flexibility into the system, they are powerless to take action. The bureaucracy becomes too powerful and unwieldy to buck.

One problem throughout much of corporate enterprise today is that managers have become so entranced by the hardware and technology, they lose sight of the basics. The business schools compound the problem. Their chief focus is on the esoteric technology centered around electronic hard and soft gadgetry, the effect being to quantify and habitualize the managerial art so that it becomes managerial drudgery. As increasing hordes of computer-bred MBAs feed into the bureaucracy, "techniques" dominate the environment. The sophisticonglomerate in its bottom-line drag race thus becomes a kind of unstoppable merry-go-round.

The poor divisional manager is lost in the spin, victimized by a system that develops quantifiers instead of managerial talent. As the technocracy is reinforced and perpetuated, the potentially creative manager, deprived of his managerial prerogatives, is turned into a robot along with the people who work under him. Subordinates know he lacks the authority to make significant decisions. So the operation becomes a robot game.

The number-identified button pusher comes in every morning, parks in the same numbered spot, greets the same numbered coworkers, goes to his same numbered cubicle, where the latest printout is waiting for him. On a prespecified date he gets his six-month review and his 6 percent increase, and goes home to his six-pack.

The Decline in Productivity—And What Is Behind It

According to Mahwah, New Jersey, management consultant Roy Walters, U.S. corporations are generally blind to the major cause of America's worrisome productivity decline.

Quoting him, Cincinnati business reporter Roy Howard Beck writes: "They're blaming government regulations, tax policies, shortage of research-and-development funding, and the lack of proper investment credits. But the biggest culprits are in the corporation's own executive suites; the most effective way to turn the decline around is to change the American style of management."*

How? By treating people like people, and managers like managers. By showing employees at all levels that you care about them.

One way is to show them consideration and respect. Ivory-tower executives in centralized isolation wards become so preoccupied with technological dig-ins to get to bottom-line pots of gold, they lose sight of basic human psychological needs. One such need is to feel important and useful, and a proven way to achieve this fulfillment is to have your ideas reviewed and accepted by the boss.

Corporate suggestion-plan managers, and human-relations and personnel experts, repeatedly counsel supervisors, in the words of one: "Even if you find an idea unacceptable for implementation for one reason or another, at least pay the suggester the courtesy and respect of seriously examining the idea, sitting down with him to explain why it's not economically feasible, and, most important, expressing your appreciation for his effort, complimenting him on whatever virtues his

* *Cincinnati Enquirer,* September 28, 1980.

73

idea might possess, and encouraging him to produce more of the same."

Apart from the human decency, this procedure makes simple common sense if you wish to keep the idea mill churning. The centralized experts often lack the interest, patience, or time to be bothered with such niceties.

In my own experience, one of my supervisors at Steelcraft came up with a leasing idea, which he spelled out in detail. He had worked hard on the plan, mostly on his own time at home. I felt it had merit and submitted it to the headquarters specialist, who had the authority to okay or reject proposed ideas that fell into his category of expertise.

Considerable time elapsed with no word from him. The supervisor was on pins and needles awaiting an answer. Seated with him at his desk in the boondocks, I called the home-office expert.

"The idea was turned down," he told me.

"Why? What did you think of it?"

He didn't have time to go into detail. He decided it wouldn't work. He wouldn't even consider it.

That was it. Thank you, Sam. Back to the printout. The supervisor looked as if his face had been slapped.

It had.

The Dismal Fate of the Maverick

"A most precious corporate asset is the spirited entrepreneur type. Corporations desperately need non-organization men. They should be humored and indulged. If the maverick is brilliant, he'll be worth 50 times what you spend on him."
—Management Consultant John Sargent*

The common everyday variety of supervisor or manager has trouble enough bearing up under remote-control decision making. But he has an easy time of it compared with the poor maverick in the centralized environment.

Of course, as Gertrude Stein might have put it, there are mavericks, and mavericks, and mavericks. I'd be the first to admit you can go overboard in humoring and velvet-gloving

---

* As quoted by Raymond Dreyfack in *Nation's Business,* February 1972.

the eccentric whose wild desires and behavior disrupt the whole organization. It reaches a point where this character can't be tolerated, no matter how bright and creative he might be. I can recall one superindividualist who insisted on coming to work garbed in varsity T-shirt and shorts. He caused such a furor, the operation came to a virtual halt. This fellow was a scientist with proven product-development talents, capable of producing a breakthrough. He was sent home nonetheless and told to reappear in more conventional array. He was insulted and quit on the spot.

"Good riddance!" his boss muttered, and I agree with the sentiment.

However, you don't have to be a nonconforming extremist to rate as a maverick. You can be a maverick and still be respectful, follow most basic rules, and not disrupt the organization.

An example comes to mind of a middle manager in corporate headquarters whose creative talents were clearly established by innovations made for a previous employer. On the basis of his track record and obvious potential, he was hired to fill a key marketing slot. Apart from his refusal to wear a white shirt or necktie, to outward appearances at least, he was fairly conventional. No wild demands on management. No irrational behavior that upset anyone or trampled peoples' sensitivities. He was, however—inordinately, in the opinion of some—attached to a cocker spaniel he owned.

This fellow had his own office with a door he could keep open or closed as he wished. One day he brought the cocker spaniel to work, took him into his office, and kept the door closed. Within minutes his boss paid him a visit. "Anderson (name disguised), what the hell do you think you're doing?"

Anderson explained. The dog had been acting unusual. He had brought him to an animal shrink, who informed him that Bubbles was depressed because he was left alone in the apartment all day. Anderson had tried a kennel, but it didn't work out. Bubbles was a sensitive dog. The only solution was to bring him to work.

"I keep my door closed. He doesn't bother anyone."

His boss shook his head. "You'll have to get rid of the dog."

Anderson balked. The boss insisted. Anderson quit in a huff. Some might side with the boss; others might say the employee's request was reasonable under the circumstances. What circumstances? The fact that Anderson was an outstandingly creative and valuable manager with a proven potential in an area of the business where such potential was in short supply and critically needed. It was also true, as the dog lover pointed out, that his behavior had little if any negative effect on the organization.

Why then was he pressured into resigning? Because in this centralized bureaucracy his insistence had a negative effect on his superior's ego. Characteristically, the boss's main concern was with control. Calling the shots, however trivial, was more important to him than achieving corporate marketing goals.

In the centralized rule-governed environment it is not uncommon for petty personal roadblocks to be erected between individual and organizational objectives. If you're a manager with your eye on the ladder, you conform to the nth degree. You don't embarrass a superior with your maverickian temperament, or even mildly diminish his power.

If you do, money-maker or not, you get zonked.

A Question of Title

I once knew a smart and savvy manager who was the president of a medium-size company that produced electrical controls and supplies. The plant was family-owned, and one day the two owners decided it was time to retire and sold out to a conglomerate. The president, whose talents and accomplishments were well known in the industry, was retained—in fact, given an increase in salary and perks—to continue running the company. He was not a member of the family.

Within weeks of the takeover a number of changes were made. One was that the president's title was changed to division manager. Another was a significant infusion of capital to expand and broaden the business. Over a period of time the ex-president and new division manager was divested of certain authorities and responsibilities in order to "standardize" corporate planning and policy. ("We're sure you understand, Jim, that we can't have division X run one way, division A run another way, and division Q run a third way.") Jim, which isn't his real name, said he understood, although he was never told why not.

At any rate, old Jim swallowed one portion of crow after another over a period of almost a year. One day he heard of a presidents' club being formed in the area, a half-business, half-social organization where presidents could exchange ideas and get away from the grind at times for an hour's conversation and relaxation at midday or in the evening. The more Jim thought of it, the more he liked the idea. It was just what he needed. He became virtually obsessed by the prospect. It became his proverbial pot at the end of the rainbow. One day, a couple of months after the club had been opened for membership and space rented, Jim submitted his application to join.

Know something? That's right, you probably guessed it. He was turned down. He wasn't a president. By now his plant employed more than a thousand people and was bigger and richer and had larger sales than three-fourths of the companies represented by the club's membership. But the proviso was a strict one: the group admitted presidents only.

That did it so far as Jim was concerned. He put feelers out in the industry and within four months found a job where he received not only the title of president but the in-charge re-sponsibility and power as well.

Now those people back in corporate headquarters on the 73rd floor who had unwittingly put down and humiliated this talented executive were not fools. Most of the top brass in that company had graduated from Harvard and other prestigious business schools, many with advanced degrees, and some at, or close to, the top of their classes. Unquestionably, they would have scored high on an IQ test.

Yet the way they deal with Jim and other high-level divisional executives is downright stupid, to state the case kindly. Why? If a person is bright, aren't dumb moves inconsistent? Not necessarily. Take this question of titles, for example. What would it have cost the corporation to have appointed Jim division president instead of division manager? Not a solitary sou that I can fathom. What, if consistency was so important, would it have cost to appoint *every* division manager president? Same answer. What would have been gained? Ask anyone who ever took Psychology I in college, and he'd have the answer at once. If you were a high-level executive and a relative, neighbor, or acquaintance asked what you did down at the plant, what would you rather tell them: that you're a manager or the president?

Is that so complex that these numbers-bred geniuses are unable to understand it? Not at all. Then what's the answer? Simply this. They're so caught up in the language of numbers, in their charts, matrixes, and computer printouts, that anyone reasoning with them in *human* language and *human* terms would never get through. He'd be "speaking in tongues," on a subject they wouldn't have time for, in an idiom that would be stranger than Greek. The trouble with these birds on the 73rd floor, unfortunately, is that too many of them are numbers-bright. But they're not people-bright.

Payoff for Loyalty, Centralized Style

The tactics of humiliation and frustration, however effective, aren't the only ways to force a good loyal manager out of the organization. Political disengagement works equally well. Unfortunately, I've seen it happen too many times, and for the victimized individual it can be a frightening and dehumanizing experience.

I'm talking about Bill Jones, 58, who started in the company as a freight clerk 23 years ago. Serious, hardworking, and conscientious, he advanced over the years from clerk to assistant supervisor to full supervisor to shipping manager. I'm sure you've run into Jones or one of his innumerable counterparts many times if you have any experience at all on the corporate scene. When he refers to the company, it's with a capital T and a capital C. The plant's goals are his personal goals. As far as Jones is concerned, the job comes first. If it's necessary to work 60 or 70 hours a week, he does so without flinching. If he's needed in the plant on Saturday or Sunday, he'll be the first to suggest it. Duty and loyalty are integral parts of his personal moral code.

In the old days this manager's dedication and performance were lauded and outspokenly appreciated by his boss, the plant manager. When distinguished visitors came to the plant, he invariably brought them over to Jones, described his operation with pride, gave his ego a much deserved boost. The warm relationship between Jones and his boss, developed over the years, came to mean a great deal to both men. Whenever the plant manager felt a promotion, special bonus, or salary increase was due, he went to bat for his loyal subordinate. Jones felt safe and secure in his job. As long as the boss was on hand to look out for his interests, as *he* looked out for the boss's interests, he had nothing to fear.

Then one day. . . . You can probably anticipate the rest of the story. With the corporate takeover of the company, an evaluation of personnel, functions, and compensation was made. Bill Jones, it was decided, was underqualified and overpaid. For one thing, he wasn't a college graduate. For another, he was behind the times so far as computer expertise was involved. For a third—though this was never revealed to Jones—the group VP had a man of his own with just the experience needed. So Jones was given three months' separation pay and let go—at age 58.

His 23 years of service, the fact that he had done a superb job for the company all those years, the reality that it would be difficult to find *anyone* who had been more loyal and dedicated to his job, counted for nought so far as the "evaluators" were concerned. When the new headquarters team took over, Bill Jones ceased being a person and overnight turned into a number. And there wasn't a damned thing the plant manager could do about it.

Admittedly, it's possible Bill Jones at 58 was a bit slower and less sharp than Bill Jones at 40 had been. Possible—but not likely. Even so, even if the company grows past the manager, as sometimes happens, you don't just discard the man if you have an ounce of humanity. You readjust his job in such a way that you will be able to use his skill and experience to the best possible advantage, and at the same time allow him to enjoy the status and security his years of faithful service warrant.

The Numbers Game

The history of business and government enterprise proves that we tend to abuse and misuse our most powerful management tools.

Example one is the typewriter. Dating back generations, as the typewriter became increasingly streamlined and efficient,

79

and as carbon copies became easier and cheaper to produce, the truckloads of paperwork mushroomed to the point where the accumulation of correspondence, memos, and reports became a major environmental pollutant. If every needless piece of paper were collected and laid end to end, the mass would stretch back and forth between New York to San Francisco a dozen times or more.

Example two is the telephone. To list all the productive and profitable applications of the telephone would require a volume the size of the Manhattan Classified Directory. By the same token, if the amount of money wasted in nonproductive telephone gabfests, and the installation and rental of excessive extensions, lines, and equipment by large organizations were donated to the American Cancer Institute, a cure for this dread disease might be discovered in weeks.

Example three is the computer. Described as "the most powerful management tool ever invented," it enhances the processing of billions of transactions, speeds research, produces in minutes information that formerly took days or weeks, eliminates countless hours of drudgery, and introduces efficiency to projects and programs previously error-ridden and chaotic. Yet, because a computer can grind out in an hour what it takes a hundred typists weeks to produce, it has turned the paper explosion into a blast that rivals Hiroshima.

More significant, runaway technology spawned by the computer has mounted a numbers-based and dehumanizing assault on the basic precepts of business and management that threatens to rob affected organizations of their spirit and dynamism. Yes, the computer, expeditiously used, can be every bit the powerful management tool its most enthusiastic proponents claim it to be. Mindlessly used, it can undermine a company and demoralize its people, which, in my experience, seems to happen more often than not, predominantly in the large centralized corporation.

According to a survey conducted some years back by a nationally known management consulting firm, computers were "ineffectively used by two-thirds of the manufacturing companies" contained in the sample. In most companies where the machines failed to pay off, the consultants found, key decisions were made by technicians rather than managers. In some cases, the technicians are called managers. But they're managers in name only, actually computermen and chartists, not businesspeople. Their orientation leans to numbers instead of functions, objectives, and people.

Still, the trend of big business is more and more to big automation, to centralized computer domains within centralized corporate realms, in which some "managers" are so highly programmed it's hard to tell them from robots.

ARITHMETIC AND THE HUMAN FACTOR

"The danger in a superprogrammed society," Raymond Dreyfack writes in *Sure Fail—The Art of Mismanagement,* "lies in the deadly social and organizational trap of Programmed Dehumanization."*

When bottom-line performance is linked more to numbers than to people, individuals tend to lose their identity. When management decisions are made exclusively by the numbers, this can breed so much efficiency that the system becomes inefficient. When that starts to happen, the programmed monster begins to devour itself. Marshall McLuhan cites GM's Lordstown operation of a decade or so back as the classic example. "Billed as the world's most automated plant," he points out, "efficiency was refined there to the dimensions of a flea's hind leg. It was a programmed miracle, a paragon of techno-scientific management. Only one thing went wrong. The operation collapsed because people wouldn't work there."†

I recently came across a centralized chemical-products company in which two giant computers at corporate headquarters, having replaced a number of smaller computers at the divisions, now controlled practically all functions ranging from manufacturing and procurement to personnel and employee benefits. Under the "total systems" system, the hiring of any nonhourly employee had to conform to a strict code of standards on a category-by-category basis as worked out by the computer.

At the height of the busy season, a production manager—one of three—quit at one of the divisions. A replacement was urgently needed, ideally a manager with industry experience. Through an almost uncanny stroke of luck, the division man-

*New York: Morrow, 1976, p. 56.
†Ibid., p. 59.

ager learned that a talented production manager employed by a major competitor was unhappy with his job and seeking a change. With a proven track record and knowledge of the company's specific manufacturing operation, this man could be slotted right into the vacancy with a minimum of orientation and break-in. The manager was contacted, interviewed, and eager to make the change. The only thing that remained was to obtain hiring approval from headquarters.

You guessed it! Approval wasn't forthcoming. Corporate hiring standards for the job in question called for "college degree, preferably master's; bachelor's degree acceptable in exceptional candidates." The man the division manager wanted to hire, although he had some years in college, had never earned his degree. "But," the executive explained to the corporate personnel officer, "he's got 14 years' experience handling the same job we are trying to fill. He's well known in this area as a manager with outstanding ability."

"If we made one exception," was the toneless reply, "we would have to make others. We have a firm policy against compromising hiring standards."

In the end the division manager had to hire, after weeks of screening and interviewing at the peak of the season, a manager who would need years of experience to become as well qualified for the job as the manager who had been rejected by headquarters. How much aggravation and irritation this computer-based decision produced would be impossible to calculate. Easier to arrive at would be the thousands of dollars lost in terms of delayed runs, production foul-ups, rework, botched-up customer orders, overtime, and training expense.

As E. T. Klassen pointed out when he was president of American Can Co.: "As we continue to increase the decisions that are suggested by computers and other devices, we are learning they possess great advantages but also some voids. There are just some things the machine cannot do, and may never be able to do for us. This is where business instinct will continue to play a major role in decision making."

There are cases where you will increase market share if you lower the price, and cases where you will increase market share if you raise the price. But I would rather rely on a businessman's instinct to guide my decision than on a computerman's numbers. When I was at Steelcraft in the pre-acquisition days,

I was told by more than one numbers man that I was crazy making the company's door the highest-priced on the market. But they swallowed their words—and their numbers—when the highest market share was achieved.

When *The Book of Lists* was in its prepublication stages at William Morrow & Co., the inevitable question of how to price the book was raised. There were those in the firm who wanted to price it out by computer. But management turned instead to a savvy and experienced senior editor, whose wise instinct prevailed. Result, the book zoomed to the best-seller lists and remained there for months.

In my experience, a computer will tell you Smith has the necessary qualifications. to head a branch in Northern Michigan. But it won't tell you he'll quit after eight months because his family hates cold weather.

A computer will tell you a need for a new product exists. But it won't tell you the product will flop in Territory 9 because the regional sales supervisor has a drinking problem and isn't doing his job.

A computer will tell you a piece of automated plant equipment will cost out to a saving of $123,698.53 per year. But it won't tell you its installation may trigger a work slowdown because employees will be worried about layoffs or regard their new role as dehumanizing.

The difference between the radically decentralized manager and the manager who worships the computer as if it were Mecca is that the RD manager takes *all* factors, and human factors in particular, into consideration when making decisions, including decisions that are aided and abetted by computers. The computer addicts, numbers-oriented and numbers-steeped, too often tend to ignore the human factor.

HIGHER EDUCATION SOMETIMES MEANS LOWER-GRADE PERFORMANCE

Corporate interviewers are growing wary of the Masters of Business Administration being turned out by the majority of business schools across the United States. As one recruitment manager states the case: "They're too expensive, too independent, and their training is usually too parochial."

Another personnel officer says, "You pay too much to get them, and then you don't keep them."

In some cash-rich corporations where the money is a secondary consideration, the growing concern is with the single-mindedness drilled into the typical MBA. The feeling might be summed up as follows:

- An overreliance on math-based techniques.
- Blue-sky career expectations plus a smug superiority that often tends to trigger resentment among lesser mortals in the organization.
- Case-history orientation engaged in by many of the business schools that too often lacks relevance to the MBA's industry, company, or functional involvement.
- Decision-making skills geared to the computer and designed to achieve short-term performance.
- A pseudo "toughness" that gives the numbers technology a higher priority than good old-fashioned human considerations.

I discussed this growing trend with two business-school educators I know who would prefer to remain nameless for obvious reasons. One replied that he agreed with every point listed above but felt the schools aren't to blame. "We merely respond to the needs and demands as they are being communicated by corporate executives."

"How many representatives of small and medium-size companies have you spoken with?" I asked.

He admitted, "None."

The other educator was even franker. "This may not be the *only* reason for the situation, but it's certainly one of the important ones. Most B schools themselves are quantitatively oriented. Our own computer printouts tell us the computer-related and numbers-based courses are the most popular and the easiest to teach."

Corporate smalls and mediums are not the only ones getting disenchanted with the current crop of MBAs, their training, and outlook. Marion S. Kellogg, vice president of General Electric Company's corporate consulting services division, observes that "people skills" are sadly lacking in many of today's MBAs. In 1980 Bank of America recruited only 79 MBA holders, down from 179 the year before. And according to *The Wall Street Journal,* "companies as diverse as International

Harvester Co. and INA Corp., the big Philadelphia insurance company, are also becoming queasy about putting freshly minted MBA holders into certain entry-level jobs. They, too, are seeking bachelor's graduates instead."*

The colleges themselves are taking note, and some are taking action as well. The University of Pittsburgh's Graduate School of Business is asking corporate executives to review their requirements. Rensselaer Polytechnic Institute offers courses for outstanding students where lecturers included members of the business community as well as faculty members. At an increasing number of business schools across the nation, business executives are being invited into classrooms to bring a real-world perception to students.†

THE RIPPLE EFFECT

Mindless decisions that disregard human feelings, needs, and preferences have a way of producing shock waves that can weaken the underpinnings of even a powerful and seemingly solid organization. It's bad enough to have key decisions taken out of the hands of operating executives on the scene by a headquarters big gun who outranks them. But to be preempted by a computer can be downright degrading.

I mentioned earlier what I consider to be one of the ultimate dehumanizations, the indiscriminate shifting around of key people from city to city and division to division without consulting them first to determine how they and their families feel about the move. If there is one thing businesspeople in this country should be ashamed of, it is this practice I have seen all too often in centralized companies. I think a concentrated effort should be made to outlaw this trading in human flesh, and if an organization is ever formed with this goal in mind, I would be proud to sign up as a member.

I have in my years of business experience in and around top management been privileged to sit in on many high-level corporate meetings, often in centralized companies. One such company with its "war room" stands out especially vividly in my mind. In this company, computer printouts were treated like biblical tomes. The only words missing at executive meet-

* February 6, 1981.
† *Business Week,* November 10, 1980.

ings, which were in essence by-products of the daily and weekly runs, were: "So spake the Lord."

A typical meeting, presided over by a somber-faced, numbers-oriented staff manager, proceeded something as follows. On a highly structured and precisely timed basis, pertinent data based on the current status of cash flow, market analysis, economic forecasts, and other "key factors" as determined by the computer would be communicated and posted to a giant "planning board." On the basis of the numbers, key-factor shifts and adjustments would be decided upon. For example:

- Open a warehouse here.
- Close down a branch there.
- Move Shaeffer from St. Louis to Minneapolis; shift Steinbrenner from Atlanta to Detroit.
- Fire Altschuler.
- Discontinue product A; step up production 30 percent on product B.

So preoccupied with the numbers were the computerniks, it would never have occurred to them to ask Shaeffer or Steinbrenner how they *felt* about relocating themselves and their families, what personal disruption the moves might entail. Nor would they consult divisional managers on the scene except summarily with regard to such decisions as warehouse openings or branch closings. So structured were most meetings I can recall, time wouldn't have been available to explore human factors and intangibles not included among the computer's inputs. Even if they'd been explored, the value might have been debatable. Managers in highly centralized and heavily computerized companies learn quickly that it is neither popular nor fruitful to dispute logic based on the printouts. In the centralized operation one usually goes along or moves along.

There's nothing wrong with computers. Without them we couldn't accomplish a lot of the things we need and want to accomplish. But they have to be handled with sensitivity and care. And there are certain things that simply shouldn't be computerized, such as dealings with customers. The customer doesn't give a damn about your computer and the benefits it might possibly give you. He wants what he wants when he wants it, and if you give him what he wants with the personal touch included, you're ahead of the game.

CRYSTALBALLMANSHIP

Centralized companies in particular tend to make a big thing of projections and forecasts. It's not surprising. The most obvious by-product activity of computerized storage and processing is to take as many key factors as you can come up with, reduce them to numbers, digest and massage them, and spit out more numbers that will tell you the shape of things to come. The only problem is that the most reliable way to predict the future is by what we know of the past. And while shoveling this into the computer is no problem, we have no guarantee that the past will be consistent with the future. It's entirely possible that new factors will develop that will invalidate one or more of the old ones.

An ancient Chinese philosopher observes: "He who could foresee affairs three days in advance would be rich for thousands of years." I wonder what comment this sage might make with regard to three-month sales forecasts, six-month economic forecasts, annual-earnings forecasts, and so on. It's been my experience that whether you call it a forecast, a prediction, or by some fancy strategic-planning label, when you estimate what you're going to do in the future, it usually adds up to a guess pure and simple, an educated guess perhaps, but a guess nonetheless.

The trouble in the centralized supercomputerized company is that the numbers boys take their guesswork seriously. They don't guess by instinct or managerial savvy. Mostly they guess by the numbers. And since you can never be sure how the numbers will tumble out during a given period, requiring a divisional manager, say, to come up with a six-month estimate is an open invitation to anxiety, because six months from now a group VP is going to walk up to this manager and say, "Hey, Charley, this is what you said would happen, and here's what actually happened." And the group VP will stand around waiting for him to say something smart.

But what can he say? Only one thing: "I guessed wrong."

So you can be pretty sure that that manager, who isn't as dumb as he looks, is going to figure out a way to estimate the market higher or lower as the case may be in order to manipulate the numbers and come out smelling sweet. Which beats most forms of anxiety.

CENTRALIZED MIND-SET—WHERE MORE THAN COMPUTERS ARE PROGRAMMED

More than a decade ago, the French author and journalist Servan-Schreiber, in his book, *The American Challenge,* tipped his hat to U.S. progressive management by categorizing it as dedicated, not merely to being, *but to becoming*—a management that focused on new ways of doing business, on developing the new concepts, methods, and procedures that are required if an organization is to stay ahead of the times.

Centralized management generally, and centralized automation in particular, militate against becoming, instead promote the status quo and encourage the inactivating condition of mind-set. It is no secret to any student of U.S. history that America was made great by its pioneers and innovators. I can't recall how many times I heard in recent months the lament from people who deplore the fallback of American enterprise, of automobiles, steel, electronic equipment, and other industries: "Whatever happened to the old entrepreneurial spirit?"

Is the age of the entrepreneur dead? I think not. Temporarily stifled by paralyzing centralization perhaps, but far from dead. In fact, the signs of revival are, in my eyes, unmistakably present. I see more and more corporations decentralizing or preparing to decentralize. I see more and more visionary businesspeople urging fellow managers to break down behemoth organizations into manageable segments headed and controlled by managers who are given the independence, freedom, and incentive to manage. I see a clear trend emerging toward the paring down and segmentation of massive government agencies and giant centralized corporations such as those in the automobile industry.

To break mind-set, you must first break the rigid superstructure controlled by electronic instead of human brains. You can refine and sophisticate strategic planning to the nth degree and beyond, and quantify every last transaction and deal. But in the end, doing business boils down to producing merchandise and service and delivering them where they are needed, when they are needed, and in the promised condition. The most impressive computer and ultra-automated plant won't mean a damn to the automobile buyer who hears a rattle in his door that turns out to be a Coke bottle some disenchanted employee stashed there.

In the end, enterprise will come down to people doing business with people. To restore entrepreneurship in America, we will have to create a climate where a manager can transact business with a customer, civic leader, or supplier who respects him because he knows he's the person in control.

THE CHINESE DID US A DISSERVICE

Paper is believed to have been invented by Ts'ai Lun in China at the beginning of the second century. Between that and gunpowder, the Chinese have been giving us problems ever since. Without paper, where would they put all the numbers? Or put another way, without numbers, how would they feed and program computers? And without computers, how could they generate such mountains of paper?

A vicious cycle that ties right into mind-set. Two of the peskiest and most troublesome problems in the U.S. today are (1) the inability of government and corporate enterprise to improve productivity sufficiently to counter inflation, and (2) environmental pollution. So far as centralized mind-set is concerned, the problems are interrelated. Centralization breeds computerization, sometimes above and beyond the call of logic and reason. Overcomputerization is to productivity in corporate enterprise what featherbedding once was to productivity in railroading. And the glut it creates is a natural by-product.

I know the former president of a food-products company that was taken over a couple of years ago by a centralized conglomerate. The parent had recently installed one of the largest, most sophisticated, ultramodern electronic data processing systems available, and one of its first moves was to tie the new division into the system. This entailed throwing out the company's small computer and auxiliary equipment and bringing in two satellite computers and remote-control linkage at a cost approximately the same as before. Headquarters "specialists" then decided what information had to be produced.

The former president, now retired, recalls being hit by an avalanche of reports and analyses that would have required a coterie of experts to review. "Not only was there more information than we could have used," my friend told me, "but not one of the reports, of itself, was complete. Each contained some pertinent information that had to be isolated from the useless data surrounding it. On top of that, the useless information, along with the pertinent material, was duplicated in report after report. A conservative estimate would be that the cost of producing the information had doubled, with its value cut in half.

Contrast this with a story I heard about a company spun off by a large centralized corporation to a medium-size decentralized conglomerate. The division had been held four years by the centralized parent, which had been unable to make it pay off. No wonder. One of the first actions the division manager took (after being promoted to president) was to request a copy of each form and report turned out by the data processing system, along with a statement explaining why the item was needed. The result was a 50 percent reduction in the amount of paperwork produced by the company—with the attendant profit improvement and work simplification that was an inevitable by-product.

THE RISING RESISTANCE TO MANAGEMENT BY THE NUMBERS

Even within the large centralized company itself the lines of battle are forming. The centralists who would integrate everything into one massive "total system" have had their way more with machines than with people. Notes Walter A. Kleinschrod, editor of *Administrative Management:* "The growing use of business minis and small 'personal' computers, often bootlegged into departments without proper authorization, could weaken the hold of data processing managers over the DP function. The rise of word processing and its ability to merge with DP only intensify the question of control and systems design."*

In my view it's time for the *real* managers, the men and women with practical management training and firing-line experience, to reassume the task of managing companies and company functions from buying and selling to hiring personnel and administering computer operations. One of the prob-

* Alvin Toffler, *The Third Wave,* New York: Morrow, 1980, p. 251.

lems I encounter repeatedly is the situation where "experts" in control are individuals trained to the teeth in techniques but woefully inexperienced in the *practices* of business. What we need if we are ever to restore productivity in America and make it zoom instead of crawl is more management practitioners and fewer theorists in top positions of influence and control.

Harvard Professor Theodore Levitt sums it up neatly: "When they attain a certain managerial altitude these days, managers need not trade what they know, and know how to do well, for the elaborate prescriptions of management-science hucksters on the make. There are only a few things worth knowing well. Underpinning them all is the truth imposed by the necessity of nature itself. Keep it simple." *

To which I say "Amen!"

The Price of Dehumanization

The impacts of supercentralization on the corporate scene are mindboggling to envision from a broad perspective. One of its saddest and most deplorable by-products is the erosion of public confidence in the U.S. corporation. As John C. Biegler, a partner in the "Big Eight" accounting firm of Price Waterhouse, states the case: "Public confidence in the American corporation is lower than at any time since the Great Depression." †

What has this to do with centralization? A great deal. Centralization, as we have seen in previous chapters and will continue to see, dehumanizes. Dehumanized managers, made victims of frustration and bitterness by their remote-control employers, are gradually reduced to a state where they care less about quality, are denied the pride of self-worth and achievement, and in self-defense become survivors instead of risk takers and leaders. When human motivations and attitudes are undermined, the inevitable result is decline, the inevitable victim the public: the customer, the consumer, the worker.

Want proof? In his book *The Third Wave,* Alvin Toffler quotes *Harvard Business Review* editor David Ewing's com-

---

* *Management Review,* April 1979.
† Alvin Toffler, *The Third Wave,* New York: Morrow, 1980, p. 251.

ment after a Harvard Business School study which reportedly "sent tremors throughout the corporate world." The study revealed that almost half of all consumers polled believe they are getting worse treatment in the marketplace than they were a decade ago; three-fifths say that products have deteriorated; over half mistrust product guarantees. Ewing notes that "public anger at corporations is beginning to well up at a frightening rate."*

Little wonder. The growing U.S. trend toward carelessly substandard workmanship—car doors that don't close, appliances that fail, clothes that don't fit properly, toys that hurt children—ranks among top concerns of responsible business leaders today. An insurance underwriter I know told me the other day that more Americans than ever before are filing liability claims—and winning large awards—in suits against manufacturers and distributors of everything from plant equipment to consumer goods.

Notes Arthur R. Taylor, a former CBS president: "There is an unfortunate rhetoric among many Americans today that whatever business wants must somehow be contrary to the best interests of the people."†

This is evidenced by the growing public anger targeted against abuses ranging from corporate price fixing and bribes to pollution of the nation's atmosphere and waterways. Never have so many outraged dissident groups been so vociferously articulate in nationwide denouncements of alleged corporate policies of underpaying workers while overcharging customers, racism in hiring and employment practices, and proliferating useless and in some cases dangerous products, all in the noble name of bottom-line performance.

Time was not so many decades ago when an independent entrepreneur could point with pride to his part and participation in the American free enterprise system. Corporate speechmakers at one time used this phrase extensively in describing the concept that made America great. The speechmaker who glowingly referred to the American free enterprise system would today in many circles be considered "behind the times." He would be scorned and derided. It is a tragic reality, be-

* Ibid., p. 250.
† Leonard H. Orr, "Why Business Got a Bad Name," *Business and Society Review,* Winter 1976.

cause, unquestionably, the American free enterprise system *is* one of the leading factors and forces—if not the outstanding force—that made America the most successful societal experiment in history.

THE GREATEST DANGER OF ALL

It's time to give a hotfoot to complacency where it exists and prevails. To state the matter as bluntly as possible, programmed dehumanization—spawned and nurtured by centralization in business and government—threatens the very underpinnings of our presumably free and independent economy. If we can point to any one thing that made America great in the past, it was the creative and innovative approach of the nation's statesmen and corporate leaders. My experience proves to me that centralization stifles the imagination. It bureaucratizes business and government. It prescribes petty strictures and mandates which, if sidestepped or violated, lay mavericks open to executive censure or worse.

Today's status-quo challenger runs the risk of getting himself caught up in a Kafkaesque maze well known to beaten path strayers in that ultracentralization of them all, the state-controlled government. Franz Kafka, in his short stories and novels—most of which were published posthumously in the 1920s, 1930s, and 1940s—depicted the working man as a hunted and harassed creature, dehumanized by the bureaucracy, his aspirations and goals thwarted by the grinding frustrations of supercentralization. He wrote with chilling clarity from years of personal experience as a clerk in the workmen's compensation division of the Austrian government. Penned well before the great holocaust, his works were a fitting prelude to the Nazi German and fascist Italian societies.

How certain can we be that "it can't happen here"? Quite frankly, I get worried at times. I know a talented manager, for example, (formerly) employed by a highly centralized corporation that shall remain nameless but whose name, if revealed, might make you gasp. A savvy marketing pro, he dared question a superior's judgment in connection with a proposed new product line.

The line was the project and dream of his boss's boss, a vice president two echelons up in the corporate hierarchy. The manager, an earnest and old-fashioned young man with the organization's best interests at heart, after studying the marketplace, competitive products, and competitive innovations in the wind, decided that developing and introducing the new product line at this time would be a disastrous move for the company to make. Honestly—and sensibly—convinced he was right, he worked long extra hours researching the subject, and submitted a comprehensive 22-page report proving and supporting his stand to his boss, who reported to the VP directly.

It would be understating this executive's reaction to say that the report scared the hell out of him. It was in his view worse than foolhardy. It was anarchy. The report, if not promptly burned, was hidden away under stacks of paper in the storeroom. Six weeks later the young manager was eased out on the pretext that a "reorganization" would soon be taking place. Seeing through the artifice, he learned the hard way that in the centralized bureaucracy one doesn't question the actions or decisions of one's superiors. Eight months later the product line was introduced and bombed horribly.

Am I being a false alarmist in fearing that centralized dehumanization in its many shapes and forms could lead to the kind of deadly authoritarian bureaucracy Kafka wrote about so eloquently? I think not. A *Time* magazine feature article states the case succinctly enough:

> One of the modern corporation's most important new challenges will be in dealing with its own employees. Karl Marx's case for Communism was based in large part on the "alienation" of industrial workers, who felt estranged from society because of the dehumanizing nature of 19th century industrial life. The overwhelming size of many modern factories and offices now makes that alienation more acute.*

It is, I believe, well past the time to take heed.

* *Time*, April 21, 1980.

CHAPTER 5

The Ravages of Remote-Control Management

It would take a special edition of *Standard & Poor's* or the *Thomas Register of U.S. Corporations* to list all the enterprises which, successful prior to acquisition by large corporations, tottered or crumbled after the takeover.

Case in point: A small-to-medium-size New York advertising agency with consecutive earnings for 23 years, forced into bankruptcy within two years of takeover. The firm long had served a specialized clientele in high-technology industries. "Too limited," was the parental verdict. When the thrust was switched to generalized services for broader-based clientele, the business gradually started to fold. On the verge of collapse, it was sold for a fraction of its acquisition price, the old philosophy reinstituted. A year later the firm was solvent again.

Case in point: Parks Sausages Inc., a highly successful meat-products manufacturer which grew from a one-man operation in 1951 to a 300-employee, $13.6 million business in 1976, suffered a 50 percent profit collapse within one year of its 1977 merger with the Norin Corporation.* In 1980, Norin in turn was swallowed by Canellus Acquisition Company, a wholly owned subsidiary of Canadian Pacific. That year, Parks registered a loss of $300,000. In November 1980, Parks was reacquired ("born again," in the words of Raymond V. Haysbert, Sr., its chief executive officer) by its original management—

* *The New York Times,* December 20, 1981.

95

and promptly started making money again. The benefits of joining a centralized conglomerate? Parks' $2 million cash reserve siphoned off by the parent; a hefty $1 million annual charge for insurance, brokerage, and other corporate services; new products introduced without proper attention to production requirements and sales potential; rising production costs and simultaneous loss of sales volume, dealt with by reducing the work force from 300 to 220; and so on.

The last two examples illustrate the "profitability cycle" mentioned earlier:

1. The company making money.
2. The company acquired by a centralized corporation.
3. The company losing money.
4. The corporation divesting itself of the company.
5. The company making money again.

The Urge to Tinker

Most big corporations acquire companies because their financial and technical experts assess them as sound operations with a good growth potential. And it stands to reason that it takes a strong and sensible management to build an organization to the point where it looks good to the evaluators. It stands to reason that if you buy a company because you think it's good, one of your major goals would be taking action—or more precisely, *refraining* from action—to keep it producing profitably. The trouble is that ego tends to rear its ugly head.

Call it Levinson's First Law if you will. The way it works is simple. The executive on the 73rd floor, the plushly carpeted part, is usually a pretty Big Guy if he has the power and authority to rule on an acquisition under consideration and say, "I like it, buy it." Less powerful, but also pretty high up is the group vice president with the mandate to control and oversee the new operation. We can assume that just as no head of a nation could ever get up there in the stratosphere without a mighty ego, neither could any corporate No. 1 or No. 2 man.

Now the nature of the egoist is that he feels he knows more than the next guy, and whatever the next guy can do, he can do it better. So you run into the situation where the following procedure takes place, proving Levinson's infallible First Law:

• A technical, financial, and special industry analysis is made of the Toledo Toothpick Manufacturing Co., with a possible eye to acquisition.

• The "experts" come in with a glowing report: good strong management, excellent quality control, good cash flow, fine reputation in the field. When better teeth are picked, they'll be picked with Toledo toothpicks.

• Corporate management negotiates with Toledo's chief executive. Both parties are amenable. The principals "hit it off." Everyone believes that one and one are going to add up to five, and the deal is made.

• Now that they own TTM, the corporate steering committee and the newly appointed group vice president sit down to study the situation in depth, and that's where the trouble starts. They look at TTM's marketing program and find it sadly lacking. They send an industrial engineering team around to assess its plant operation and come up with the finding that it's getting only 53.765 percent productivity. They bring in technical consultants who mike up the toothpicks and find the dimensions all wrong and the wood too hard. Accounts receivable don't come in fast enough; accounts payable are shelled out too fast.

• A decision is made to "restructure" the newly acquired company. In my dictionary, thats a synonym for "tinker."

An executive can tinker within the confines of his own department, division, or company. Or he can tinker on a remote-control basis. Hundreds of large U.S. corporations today have mushroomed into multiindustry, multidivision, multilocational structures. Close personal relationships between high-level executives in corporate headquarters and division heads in Biloxi, Frog's Gulch, or Weehauken rarely exist, so it's no wonder faith and trust are missing. To establish control, profit centers are set up, strategic-planning units developed, with layers of management formed in the towers to keep tight reign on the octopal arms. These managers run a fast track where the scoreboard registers winners and losers in the language of numbers.

The only way to juggle numbers is to tinker with them. And tinkering is as natural to centralized corporate management as betting is to the gambler.

Theoretically, and in some cases practically, getting acquired by a big rich company is supposed to put an end to scrimping and scrounging for funds needed to finance worthwhile programs and projects. In one company I know of, a line of medical analyzers and pumps introduced the year before showed particular promise and growth potential. The general manager, the manufacturing vice president, and the production manager worked together for weeks to come up with a viable, realistic, and practical expansion plan that would require a near-term expenditure of $250,000. A three-page report summarizing the highlights of the plan was submitted to the corporate controller at headquarters. In response, a meeting was called that tied up division executives at the Cleveland main office for almost three days.

Scores of questions were fired at the general manager and his people by the controller and his budgeting experts. In the end, the plan was turned down pending the submission of more information "critically needed to evaluate the proposal."

"In pre-acquisition days," the general manager remarked bitterly, "we'd apply to the bank for a loan. The bankers, who didn't know us from Adam, required only a fraction of the data we've been ordered to supply. And we were never turned down."

MOTIVATING THE TROOPS

Another ego trip Club 73 executives too often take is based on their conviction that as managers of The Corporation headquartered in the Big City, they know more about motivating employees than those hicks out in the boondocks—despite the fact that the hicks have been running a successful operation for years, and that the hick executives have been working with and living with their key people for years. There are more people-related management problems—and more problem managers—than you could fit into a ten-ton trailer truck. And I'm not talking about managers who aren't qualified to manage. I'm talking about talented men and women who do a bang-up job but need special and delicate treatment. Manager A has bureaucratic leanings if you don't keep him on track. Manager B is a "crisis manager" unless he is given proper guidance. Manager C is a loner—put him off by himself and he's a pro, work him in with a team and he becomes ineffective. Manager D quickly grows frustrated if he doesn't get good visibility. And so it goes on and on and on.

The likelihood that a Club 73er is better qualified and equipped to handle and motivate these people than the executive on the scene, who knows them not merely as functions and number producers but as *people,* is about as strong as Jane Fonda running for the Senate on a conservative ticket.

It would be impossible to document, of course, but interesting to know, how many large corporations are running companies and divisions remotely—and running them down because of insensitivity to the human factor and to business needs that could be more effectively fulfilled on the local level by experienced operating managers. I suspect a list at least as long as a typical North Dakota telephone directory could be compiled. In my experience, the more heterogeneous an organization becomes, the tougher it gets to cope with the problems and complexities of its diverse operations.

Management consultant Peter Drucker echoes this contention. He says: "What we really need is for a company to see that one of its undermanaged, underexploited activities is really big enough to run itself, and then spin it off as an independent business. I could name 75 places where a business with volume ranging from $50 million to $300 million could be created if the big companies could divest and get out. I'm convinced that we'll have to come to that."*

THE THEORY OF FRESH PERSPECTIVES

An interesting method of tinkering is to turn over an engineering problem or project to an advertising executive. "How's that?" you ask. By what stretch of the imagination is an ad man qualified to tackle an engineering task?

Exactly!

But there's a rationale that endorses this approach, and it isn't all nutcake. Let me cite an example.

An Ohio producer of metal shelving, desks, cabinets, benches, and other shop and office products was owned by a Chicago-based conglomerate. The parent company's chief executive liked to look upon himself as a creative and imaginative manager. He railed against narrow and limited thinking.

---

* *Business Week,* October 17, 1970.

One of his favorite precepts was The Theory of Fresh Perspectives.

In a nutshell, what this amounted to was bringing new approaches, philosophies, and viewpoints to bear on problems, projects, and programs. A laudable concept in principle, and fruitful where exercised rationally. But one that can easily deteriorate into costly tinkering if carried to unsound extremes.

In this case the metal-products division, which had been operating successfully for almost half a century, had initiated a program to update its product line, discontinue certain unprofitable units, expand production on others, and add selected new items. The program was launched with the parent company's blessing. The chief executive, who believed in keeping a tight rein on subsidiaries and was something of a bug on personal involvement, gave the division people just one proviso: the revised product mix would have to be okayed by him on what amounted to a unit-by-unit basis. Another of the chief's characteristics—or eccentricities—was the spouting of corporate axioms. One of his favorites was the quote credited to Andrew Carnegie about the great manager being the man who knows how to surround himself with men much abler than himself.

The chief believed in his people, possibly because he rarely allowed his people to make important decisions without his supervision and approval. Whatever the case, combining the Carnegie axiom with The Theory of Fresh Perspectives triggered a brainstorm I've seen duplicated time and again in various corporate suites. The chief decided to bring "diverse and multidisciplined thinking" to bear on the selection of the division's product mix.

Specifically, when the rough dummied catalog sheets were submitted for parental approval, he assembled the corporate marketing vice president, financial vice president, head of the legal department, vice president of manufacturing, transportation manager, data processing director, and his secretary in the conference room to review them. Beaming munificently, the chief polled the assemblage of men and women presumably, and very possibly, more able than he was. Each executive as well as his secretary felt compelled to contribute some thinking on a subject he or she knew nothing about. The ad executive passing judgment on the engineering program.

100

Needless to say, the chief's opinion outranked all others. Though he was no more qualified than his aides to evaluate the division's product line, he was influenced by superficial "contributions" from managers whose judgment was influenced by a host of factors ranging from computer printouts and the numbers on financial statements to regional trends and the law. The final outcome, as you can well imagine, was a mess: items chopped that were critical to customer service and profit performance, units added for the most harebrained of reasons.

Not surprisingly, the tinker-toy division's sales and earnings plummeted in years to come. The operation was sold off at a loss, with a gradual recovery reported only after its original management control was restored and the tinkering damage undone.

Incredible? Perhaps. But it happens every day in the far reaches of Tinkerland. Give a child a man's toy to play with and he will probably break it.

A NATION OF TINKERMAN

It has been my observation that the centralized corporation, which encompasses the greater segment of corporate enterprise in America, propogates two kinds of tinkermen: the captive tinkerer and the willful or voluntary tinkerer.

The captive tinkerer tinkers because he's expected to tinker, or invited to tinker, by his boss. As in the case cited above, when the boss comes over and asks, "What do you think about this?" or "What do you think we should do?" it's an invitation to tinker, one the subordinate manager can't very well sidestep. If, as too often happens, he's not the right person to answer the question or pass judgment on the issue, he will still very naturally think twice before replying, "I don't know," or "I'm not qualified on that subject." After all, who needs unqualified people around? More likely, he'll rack his brain for some kind of a sensible-sounding response, or reply, "Let me give that some thought."

Whatever the case, the captive tinkerer tinkers because he has no other choice; he's been set out on a tinkering limb.

The willful tinkerer tinkers because it's his nature to tinker, he's been conditioned to tinker, or the nature of his job makes him a tinkerer. He doesn't think of what he's doing as tinkering; he thinks of it as doing his job and, hopefully, getting ahead in the process. He equates tinkering with getting ahead. If he tinkers, he's "aggressive." If he butts out, he is "passive." Passivity gets you no place. Aggressiveness sparks high-level attention and, with good luck, plaudits, recognition, and credit.

We are philosophically and organizationally geared to produce a nation of tinkermen. Consider the following factors:

Academic grounding. American business schools train students to tinker by stressing mathematical and computer-based skills rather than the everyday problems of making the product, meeting the payroll, motivating employees, and keeping customers satisfied. The numbers-oriented MBAs end up in headquarters suites, the real managers in division factories and offices. The problems start when the MBAs interfere in the operational decisions of the division people.

Guidelines and manuals. Tinkering by the book is standard procedure in most large corporations. One major difference between the centralized and the decentralized organization is that for a great many functions and activities—hiring, pensions, labor relations, compensation, purchasing, and so on—the centralized corporation publishes one book that applies for all divisions, whereas the decentralized corporation permits each division to tailor its own set of guidelines and policy statements to its individual needs. When a company is taken over by a centralized parent, the standardized guidelines invariably conflict with existing rules and procedures. It would be impossible to estimate the amount of friction and frustration this creates in the division, not to mention the waste of money and time.

Fiefdoms. A corporate fiefdom, once created and rooted, can be harder to break down than a politically inspired government agency. For example, in a centralized conglomerate it's not unusual for a corporate marketing vice president to have a staff of 50 or 60 people reporting to him—research people, mathematicians, economists, computer experts, statisticians, and support personnel. Each one of these bodies must be justified, along with each study, survey, and program initiated. More often than not, the end result of each study, survey, and program is tinkering.

102

Risk-Free Management

Is there any way to come out with a new product and be sure it is going to succeed? Can you come up with a formula for going into a joint venture with the assurance that you're going to make money? Do you know how to hire a key executive and be certain he's going to do a good job?

If your answer is yes to any of these questions, you're either a wishful thinker or a magician. Risk-free management doesn't exist. Every management decision you make is a gamble. It may work; it may not. If you hit pay dirt 50 percent of the time, you're probably doing all right. If you hit 60 percent or more of the time, you're riding high on the hog.

The numbers boys, from what I have seen, are trying to perform an impossible feat; they're trying to take the risk out of management. They're using computer printouts to pragmatize and rationalize management decisions. Theoretically, they are often successful. Practically, it can't be done.

Theoretically, you can quantify a bunch of computer inputs and outputs, formularize a marketing or financial strategy, and, mathematically, make A plus B equal C. Practically, it usually doesn't work out, because you can't quantify a customer's emotional response when a delivery doesn't get there on time, or a manager's gut feeling that gilt-edged curtain rods won't sell in Vermont, or a sales rep's bitterness when he's transferred against his will to Blissful Creek, Mississippi. You can't quantify the human factor. You can't calculate or formularize the human factor out of existence. And you can't take the risk out of business.

One day when I was at American Standard I paid a call on Sears Roebuck and was told that Sears was ready to buy $1 million worth of doors if we were interested. I was assured by my contact at Sears that the company wanted very much to do business with us. Needless to say, my sales department at Steelcraft was excited. It couldn't wait for me to come back with the contract.

I returned to Sears, where the contract was quickly prepared. All that remained, I was told, was the formality of signing the chain's standard purchase agreement. Following corporate procedure, I submitted this to American Standard's legal department.

"Uh, uh," I was told. "No way! We can't sign this contract."

"Why not?"

"It says here that if anyone ever gets hit by a door, a liability would result, and that Sears would be absolved from the liability; the liability would be American Standard's. Sorry, Levinson, no deal."

I went back to Sears and they were devastated. They really wanted those doors. But no less locked into the corporate rule book than American Standard, they had no way to bypass that ironclad clause. They suggested that their legal department get together with our legal department. That was done. Still no contract.

Now what's the chance of anyone getting hit by a door, or having a door dropped on his head? It's conceivable, of course. A careless person can walk into a door; he can catch his foot in a door. Accidents happen, and lawsuits can result. But to what extent do you go to avoid liability? How foolproof can it be to do business?

I went to the president of American Standard. We talked about it and decided that the possibility of being sued by someone who was hurt by a door was a business risk, and that it was a gamble worth taking. He overrode the legal department and let me make the decision. I took the order and everybody was happy, even the legal department, because the buck had been passed. But I couldn't help wondering: How many good deals are thwarted, how many creative plans are stymied, how much profit is washed down the drain, how many managers frustrated and driven to seek other jobs, because of tinkerers trying to play it so safe they block growth and progress instead? It's a thought to take with you.

"We are Driven!"

You probably recognize this as Datsun Motor Co.'s hard-hitting slogan. Well, it may work for an automobile manufacturer whose sales focus is driving down prices. But it won't work for people in general and executives in particular.

A characteristic not necessarily unique to, but certainly predominant among, highly centralized multidivisional corporations is the pressure-cooker syndrome. In these companies, the operational word is PERFORMANCE, and performance, however adequate, is rarely adequate enough.

THE 8 PERCENT SELLOUT

Here's the problem in a nutshell from its ivory-tower origins. Group vice president Spindelhoffer, who daily recites a numerically coded version of the Lord's Prayer and kneels in silent tribute to the computer, supervises five divisions of a New York-based conglomerate. One day his boss, the president, B. L. (Bottom Line) Quackenbush, approaches him with a grim look on his face. "Spin, Division B isn't attaining its full potential. It's been holding firm at 8 percent profit when it should be hitting 12 percent at least."

"But, B. L.—"

Spindelhoffer's "but" is butted head-on by the latest computer printout headed: MARKET PROJECTION—DIVISION B. The report spells out "optimum product mix," "achievable market share," "calculated cash flow," and other key indicators, factors the figures on an input-output cost-control matrix, and winds up with a bottom-line potential profit projection of 12.01354 percent. This leaves Spindelhoffer tongue-tied. Having climbed to a group VP slot in the company, he knows what it takes to survive: *you don't argue with the computer.* Nor do you argue with B. L. Quackenbush. Spindelhoffer's work is cut out for him, and he knows what it is. He reads B. L.'s cool electronic stare to mean, "Achieve Division B's 12 percent potential, or I'll find someone who can."

Spindelhoffer, caught between the proverbial rock and a hard place, leaves that meeting with the chief thinking, my job hinges on whether I can make 12 percent or not. Not surprisingly, his orientation is not, how can I make Division B grow and develop into a strong, solid organization for the long pull, but what steps can I take to boost current profits from 8 percent to 12 percent now, regardless of the future—the 8 percent sellout. His goal now is no longer *company*-oriented; it is Spindelhoffer-oriented. He's fighting for his job, for his life, for survival.

Now let's carry our little melodrama a step further. Spindelhoffer, fired with new resolution—which he figures is better than being fired, period—flies out to Peoria for an inspirational chat with Charley Brokenbak, Division B's operating vice president.

"Charley," he says, "I've got good news for you."

He shows him the computer projection. "Isn't that great? We can boost profits 50 percent. That's outstanding growth potential. It says so right here in black and white."

Brokenbak, chalk-white to begin with at the prospect of Spindelhoffer's visit, pales two shades. "But Spin, I've been in this business 24 years. I know what it costs to run this plant; I know what the market will yield."

He calls in his controller, his manufacturing guy, and his marketing man. They blanch at the suggestion that profits can be boosted from 8 to 12 percent.

Undaunted, Spindelhoffer shows them the printout. "You guys can do it. Look, it says here . . ."

The Peoria boys, like Spindelhoffer, know enough not to argue with the computer printout, even if they understood what the labels, projections, and indicators were all about. After all, they have families too, mortgages, boats, youngsters in college, and other obligations.

Spindelhoffer flies back to New York feeling better than when he flew out to Peoria. The boys will come through for him. He has no idea how, but one way or other they'll make it. And he's right.

But at what cost success? Costs will be axed to the bone. Advertising and promotion will be cut back to a fraction. The sales staff will be reduced. Research and development will be chopped in half.

The result? Profits for this year will rocket. B. L. Quackenbush will pat Spindelhoffer paternally on the back, present him with a nice bonus check, and tell him, "Spin, I knew you could do it."

Charley Brokenbak will get similar treatment.

"This year's picture at Division B," Quackenbush will tell the beaming board of directors, "looks better than it ever has in the past."

What about next year, and the year after that? Hmmmm. We don't talk about that.

The short-term perspective should come as no surprise, states Lester C. Thurow, professor of economics and management at the Massachusetts Institute of Technology:

American managers are looking over their shoulders at investors who invest on a daily if not hourly basis. Top management is given a bonus based on current profits. Middle-level management has been organized into independent profit centers where people are promoted or demoted based on current profits. New MBA's are implicitly taught that the short-run bottom line is the only thing. With that structure of incentives anything but a short time horizon would be a miracle. And there are no economic miracles.*

THE "GOTCHA" SYNDROME

The "gotcha" syndrome starts with the divisional plan and budget submitted to corporate headquarters for approval. In addition to spelling out projected actions and goals, the plan must be documented by quantitative support material relating anticipated functions, moves, and investments to the bottom line on a detailed basis. After the material is reviewed by the experts at headquarters, a meeting is set up with the division manager and possibly one or two of his aides. At the meeting the nit-picking gets under way.

> "You said you were going to increase your market share 2 percent two years ago, and another 3 percent last year. But that's not what you did."

You could go into a discussion explaining that certain materials became unexpectedly scarce, energy costs rose 15 percent, and a wildcat strike was called at the plant. But the numbers boys don't want to know about that. It says here you were supposed to do this or that, and you didn't do it.
Gotcha!

> "On page eight of your report, you projected a targeted cost reduction of 18 to 20 percent. The actual figure came to less than 13 percent."

Thirteen, you might explain, was a monumental achievement. You might further explain that the 18 to 20 percent reduction wasn't your idea to begin with. But it wouldn't do any good.
Gotcha!

> "On page eleven you deal with eliminating unprofitable items from the product line. Yet we see here that the following items

* *The New York Times,* February 8, 1981.

107

are marginal and being retained, and three items are actually producing a loss."

The answer is that, loss or not, if you discontinued those items, customers would turn elsewhere for them, and for other items as well. But that's not factorable by the computer, so there'd be no point in discussing it.

Gotcha!

So it goes. Detail after detail they pore over the sheets and figures, gloating visibly over the power they possess to make you squirm and cringe. You're like Johnnie coming to Teacher with your composition. Teacher scrutinizes your work for a scratch mark here, a wrong word there, an erasure somewhere else, constantly searching for "gotchas" while you're supposed to be meekly and worrisomely sitting there on the griddle.

In my view, I submit, that's not the way to do business with people who are presumably equals or near-equals. You don't win the cooperation, friendship, loyalty, and dedication of others by browbeating them and putting them down. If you trust them sufficiently to conduct business for you at a remote place and in your absence, if you had enough faith in their business savvy and judgment to buy the operation in the first place, you should have enough confidence, faith, and re-spect to allow them to do business the way their experience, instinct, and intelligence tell them is the best way to do busi-ness. And to hell with the computer!

The only thing the "gotchas" accomplish is to get to you.

DRINK ISN'T THE ONLY THING YOU CAN DRIVE A MAN TO

Psychologists and sociologists who study such things tell us that by nature, inherently, most people are honest. But push a person against a wall to the point where his job is in jeop-ardy, where there's a threat that his mortgage won't be met or that he may have to pull a son out of college because he can't pay the tuition, and there is no telling how he'll react.

Wall pushing is a favorite pastime of the school of remote-control management. Like the "domino theory," the process moves right down the line starting on the 73rd floor, filters down to the 72nd, and all the way out to the boondocks. The further down the line it goes, the more routine and mechanical wall pushing becomes, because the more depersonalized it becomes. The Top Domino is wall-pushed by the stockholders and board if, as so often occurs, they happen to have a heavy foot on the pedal called PERFORMANCE. Number-two Domino is tougher than rail spikes and has a hungry eye on the top spot. It's not too hard for him to pass the profit message along down to the 72nd floor. From there it is carried along to the divisions, bridging the gap between operations and staff, and inevitably reaching the manager responsible for cutting costs on production, boosting sales volume, and squeezing better productivity out of workers.

Whatever syrupy words and inspirational hip-hoorays the message may include, two unspoken words are often implicit: OR ELSE! These are the words, directly or indirectly intimated, that change honest men into crooks, individuals who seek a fair and honorable place in the sun into people who fudge and cheat in the shade. More often than not, they fudge and cheat, not because they are greedy, although this is sometimes the case, but because, forced up against that hard cold wall, they are fighting for their lives.

Here is just one of many cases I've come across. A supermarket manager was pushed for a profit yield which he knew wasn't there. He knew something else, too, from the visiting delegate's ultimatum. If he didn't make the figures specified, he wouldn't be there either. He made them. He marked up selected prices outrageously and illegally; he taught his girls how to cheat at the cash registers; he fudged the figures like a blind juggler. The only thing he bought was time, which was the best he could hope for—time to shop around for a new job, preferably in a new industry as well. He found what he wanted eight months later, left the store in a hopeless mess that took half a year to clean up, and left personnel who had by now acquired sophisticated expertise in how to cheat, not only customers but management as well.

Sad legends of this kind could go on and on and on. We have seen a growing number of indictments in recent years, such as in the American Can Co. (Sam Goody) case, where two executives where charged with selling counterfeit recordings or returning fake copies for refund to legitimate suppliers; where division managers of H. J. Heinz Co. falsified accounts to show the profit they were ordered to make; where a Chase

Manhattan Bank bond officer was indicted for doing pretty much the same thing.

Notes a *Business Week* editorial:

> In the diversified corporation run by financial people who have no feel for the fiber and texture of a business, the bottom line is all that matters. They manage the bottom line to produce a desired number of dollars in profit, and then they order division executives to produce their share—or else. The door is opened for shenanigans that the top management doesn't expect and cannot curtail because it doesn't understand the business.*

Human beings the world over act no less than human. If a person feels his head is on the block, if the survival of his job or division is at stake, he will all too often throw not only caution but ethical standards as well to the wind.

The Feeble Giant

"In practically all of our activities," the chief executive complained, "we seem to suffer from the inertia resulting from our great size. It seems to be hard for us to get action . . . there are so many people involved."

Is this familiar lament from the head of one of today's giant international multidivisional conglomerates? It well might be, but actually it was an introspective evaluation of the state of the corporation made by General Motors' Alfred P. Sloan, Jr., in 1925, when the company's personnel roster was a small fraction of its current payroll of about three-quarters of a million people.†

Why this persistent worry and concern over size, by Alfred P. Sloan, Jr., in the 1920s, and by scores of corporate leaders today in the 1980s, six decades later? One explanation involves flexibility. Just as the human animal who is grossly overweight moves with slowness and difficulty, the oversized corporate animal's actions and responses tend to profit-crippling lethargy. Another point against size in the unwieldy centralized corporation is management's predilection toward rational

---

* Business Week, March 17, 1980.
†*Business Week,* October 17, 1970.

(often computerized) decision support, as opposed to human judgment and instinct.

"Uncertainty," states New York University Graduate School of Business professor Zenas Block, "is anathema to giant corporations. Once a company is securely entrenched in its markets, uncertainty gives way to control, predictability, and institutionalization—priorities that its managers, products of the schools of business administration, are trained to enforce." *

Innumerable tales could be told of brilliant entrepreneurs who founded, nourished, and developed small enterprises and watched them prosper and grow over the years, until, lo and behold, they found themselves with unmanageable monsters on their hands. One such story, some Wall Streeters are speculating these days, involves Wang Laboratories, long a fair-haired favorite of the investment community.

While many American companies today are struggling to survive, Chinese-born inventive genius An Wang's problem is how to avoid expanding his enterprise out of control. The company's growth, always impressive, has been little short of spectacular during the past four years. Its work force, a mere 1,000 just a decade ago, now runs 14,000 or so. Expanding at a staggering 67-percent annual rate since 1977, the company is considering drastic steps to keep from bursting its corporate seams.

"It's impossible to maintain efficiency with growth at this dizzying pace," a New York-based investment analyst contends. "Something has to give, and probably will without a firm hand on the reins." †

Something already is giving, some industry watchers believe. Customers are beginning to complain about service snags in Wang's word-processor and small-computer divisions. One reason for this is the company's inability to train and develop field and customer support personnel fast enough to keep up with the workload. Another reason, one former Wangsman confides, relates to the organization's centralized structure. The company's divisions are closely controlled by the parent on a functional basis. The problems are clear to most divisional

---

* *The New York Times,* February 15, 1981.

† Art Pine, "Firm with a Growing Problem," *Washington Post News Service,* February 1981.

managers, the informant feels, but they are powerless to make corrective decisions.

The big-is beautiful business philosophy has long been a tough nut to crack. Youth and its go-go impetus are a factor, of course. In most large corporations, telling the young go-getters to slow down would be like telling a gull to stop diving for fish. No matter how often critics urge managers to keep growth size under control, states New Jersey educator and management consultant Leonard J. Smith, all indications point to the growth frenzy remaining an unalterable fact of business life.

Another factor is the business-school brainwashing geared to bottom-line performance today, with each day's, week's, and month's performance measured against the prior period on an ongoing basis. Smith believes that managers equate size with success, whether it's a department, division, or corporation.

As The Conference Board's Wilbur McFeely once stated the case: "A large organization really lives on momentum rather than vitality."

Unless it is radically decentralized! Radically decentralizing the corporate giant immediately converts it from a sprawling, inflexible, waste-ridden and lumbering entity to an organization composed of 10, 20, or 50 fast-moving and decisive small business entities—provided, of course, that capable divisional managers are on hand to do the job that needs to be done.

CORPORATE INDIGESTION

It is ironic that in the automobile industry, which in its early days helped to spawn and implement the concept of decentralization, the need for radical decentralization these days is especially acute. Why was it, asks Florida consultant Arthur Burck, that when two decades ago so many businesspeople, consumers, and indeed world car-industry leaders as well, were able to visualize so clearly the urgent need for small cars, managers in Detroit not only missed the boat but didn't even show up at the dock? Were they myopic, he asks, stupid, ostrichlike, or plain greedy? Maybe some or all of these things, he replies, but it is unthinkable that a whole sophisticated industry could be ill-managed for so long. Here is his explanation:

The simple reality is that the Detroit managers had no choice. They were locked into a situation that resulted from the concentrated structure of the industry: one behemoth and two giants. With countless billions tied up in plants, tools, dies, and products that would become obsolete with a drastic size change, managers naturally resisted steps that would jeopardize the huge investment, especially since large cars were so profitable and there was no real threat (or so they thought) from domestic or foreign competitors.*

An organization can be hogtied by size as surely as it can be thwarted by changing marketplace preferences and competitive innovations. It is interesting to note that in recent years several of the most vulnerable victims to become prey to foreign competitive invasion have been the mammoth corporations, U.S. Steel Corporation with assets of $11 billion as one glaring example.

Burck's solution: a national policy that discourages mergers between commercial or industrial giants, and the deconcentration of industries where insufficient competition exists. "Breaking up companies is not as harsh a remedy as everyone thinks," he contends. "Indeed, stockholders will invariably benefit. Why? Today's economic reality is that the parts of most huge underperforming companies are worth much more than the whole. . . ."

In my experience this is triply true of the divisions of the heavily centralized corporation. Today, more than ever before, in the face of growing competition from abroad, in many key U.S. industries the nimbleness and flexibility that only radical decentralization can provide are more critically needed than ever.

LEVINSON'S LAW OF DISECONOMY

Simply expressed, Levinson's Law of Diseconomy goes as follows: *Now you see it; now you don't!*

It applies to the fallacious economy-of-scale concept so popular among the centralized giants. Conceptually it is easy to make a sound and convincing case for centralized management in general and centralized buying in particular. Buy in

---

* Business Week, November 17, 1980.

large quantities and you're in a more favorable negotiating position, you get a better deal, and you buy for less.

So the argument goes.

Levinson's Law of Diseconomy challenges this widely held contention. "Now you see it" means that economy of scale sounds obvious and logical when it is spelled out in advance. "Now you don't" means that nine times out of ten, taking action on this premise results in a loss in the end.

While there are certainly exceptions to this law, as there are to all good laws, the reasons for its creation are sound and basic. Here they are:

1. There are hidden costs you incur through centralized buying. Materials must be stored, involving labor, overhead, and "shrinkage" due to loss, damage, and deterioration. Storage at a central location usually means shipment to points of use. In many large corporations, centralized purchasing tends to create a minibureaucracy within the maxibureaucracy, with all the extra paper shuffling and employment this condition inevitably generates, all of which I refer to as the "fatness curve."

2. It takes extra time and effort to track down special quantity deals, if indeed such deals exist. The fact of life is that in many industries they don't.

3. Quantity purchasing often implies standardization, beneficial in theory, but sometimes disadvantageous in practice. Individual users frequently sacrifice convenience, quality performance, or operating effectiveness in adjusting to standards, not to mention the out-of-pocket cost of adjustment. Sometimes the sacrifice cost exceeds the value of the saving.

4. Some bargains aren't bargains at all. Example: You make a deal with Hertz to get 20 percent off on quantity usage of car rentals. Then you find out that the cost, *with* the 20 percent discount, is greater than the regular cost of one of the budget rental car services.

5. People often have a tendency to order and/or use more of an item if it is bought at a so-called discount, or bargain, price.

6. A common argument for centralized quantity purchasing is that it gives you more clout with the vendor. Actually, it gives you *less* clout in many cases, because smart vendors prefer dealing with several smaller buyers that exercise less

control on the one hand, without creating substantial shakeup and loss in the event of withdrawal on the other.

7. In times of shortage, large buyers often exert undue pressure to get vendors to commit an inordinate percentage of available stock, a practice that antagonizes smaller customers and creates all kinds of problems.

8. Persuading a vendor to give you a special price advantage based on quantity usually obligates you to buy all or most of your supply from this source, a risky practice in business. I could cite more than one instance where, at the height of its busy season, a buyer's source suddenly ran dry because of a vendor fire or strike.

9. More than once I have seen vendors, suddenly apprehensive over the degree of domination exercised by a large buyer, regret the deal that was made, or realize that the bargain offered was so much of a bargain it squeezed profit margins too hard. In one case a liquor distributor stopped selling to its highest-volume customer, a giant department store, because a combination of special concessions offered, plus the store's strategy of using the wholesaler as an independently owned warehouse, resulted in a net loss instead of a gain. Too often, where a special deal creates marginal profits or aggravation for the vendor, there is a gradual conversion from reliable to unreliable supplier.

10. Small or moderate buying offers advantages quantity buying is often unable to match. A key factor is the added flexibility. A big deal ties you down to specific terms and commitments. When special opportunities to make a better deal arise unexpectedly due to a vendor's unique needs or changing market conditions, you may be unable to seize them. I can recall one situation where, as a moderate buyer, I was able to buy merchandise in advance almost at cost because the vendor was in a cash bind and needed the quick payment I was able to offer.

11. There is no question that uniformity is the hallmark of the large centralized corporation and its purchasing function. The whole procurement procedure is usually bogged down by cumbersome paperwork and endless routine. It has been my experience that uniformity erodes not only human enthusiasm but profitability as well.

12. "Footsie," unfortunately, is a popular game a minority

of purchasing executives play with vendor sales reps. The larger the orders, the higher the stakes, the greater the temptation. There's nothing like regularly audited competitive bids from a reasonable sampling of suppliers to keep the purchasing operation above-board and square.

"But, Hey, How About All Those Wonderful Services?"

From the centralized perspective, big isn't only beautiful, it's a treasure chest of sophisticated expertise as well, and Mr. or Ms. divisional manager, it is yours for the asking. Or is it?

A question often raised when decentralization is being considered involves the rash of services usually offered by Big Daddy to the divisions. These range from marketing and pricing consultation to research and development, data processing, and compensation. The worry is: "Aren't we going to miss them?" But let's look at some of the offerings more closely from a real-world point of view. Here are three case histories randomly selected from a source file of dozens.

Case 1—Research and Development: The company in question produced a line of rope and sling products, all manufactured in compliance with OSHA standards. Acquired about three years ago, it became a division of an Illinois-based conglomerate. The unit had a compact, highly competent research staff, which had operated successfully for several years and had created many new products that had gained wide market acceptance. Enter Big Daddy on the scene with his offer of "R&D consultation and assistance." Translation: "From now on we'll make the decisions."

Result: almost immediately the centralized Sure Thing Syndrome came into play. In the past, some of the division's good ideas, and its one most profitable idea, were somewhat unconventional by established industry standards. That no longer goes. Headquarters R&D staffers subject proposed ideas to "scientific evaluation," usually computer-based. And telling a computer "unconventional" is like recommending a chiropractor to your neighborhood orthopedist. The trick is to minimize risk taking, a feat I have as yet to see succeed.

Result: inevitable hangups and bogdowns. Central R&D, with approximately 32 divisions to service, has a continuing scheduling problem on its hands. Thus a not surprising scenario shows divisional product researchers in a race with competitive researchers to develop a new product in response to market needs and coming up with a hoped-for winner. But by the time the proposed winner gets reviewed, refined, and approved by the headquarters experts, a competitor's new product is already on the market.

Case 2—Patents and Trademarks: In the "good old days" patent and trademark problems and needs were handled by a local patent attorney in this small to medium-size medical-supplies company. The attorney knew the people and, after years of experience with the client, understood their problems and needs.

Today the company, now a division, must turn to Daddy's in-house legal department instead of the local attorney. Prior to tackling a problem, the corporate lawyers must undergo what amounts to a virtual training and orientation program. With a host of divisions to service, this program will be reenacted every time a patent problem arises.

One inevitable consequence is costly delay, which wrecks development and production schedules. The home-office lawyers have their own problems to contend with: at last report, a heavy backlog of assignments from several divisions with no light at the end of the tunnel. From the division manager's viewpoint, the "savings" are hardly impressive.

Case 3—Computer Services: In this large apparel manufacturer, inventory and sales orders were centralized on a large home-office computer. Forty-one divisions and subsidiary units were slated to be serviced by Big Daddy. The instructions were simple and straightforward enough: "You get rid of your computers and put in terminals instead. You'll save a pile." The old story.

Instead of saving a pile the result was a pileup. The old traffic problem and competition among the 41 units for computer time was only part of the headache that evolved. Under the old setup, when the sales manager, production manager, or controller requested a special report or a weekly or monthly report, the data processing manager was hard pressed to produce it. The reason: computer time was expensive and at a premium. As a result executives thought twice, then once again, before requisitioning printouts. It worked out much better than one might imagine. Reports that were genuinely needed to make key decisions and run the business had a way of getting produced. The fringe stuff, frivolously or thoughtlessly requested, was automatically eliminated by the system.

No more. The new rationale goes as follows: "Hey, we've got this new giant computer at our disposal. We can get all kinds of fancy reports just for the asking."

With the floodgates opened from 41 units, you can imagine the consequence. The headquarters computer experts are poorly qualified to determine what is actually needed and what the division could just as well live without. The consequence is confusion and backlogs compounding further confusion, with the giant computer growing more massive and monstrous each day so that the corporation is now in danger of having magnetic tape streaming out of its windows and doors. At last count 41 programmers were employed, ironically one for each unit.

This isn't to say that all centralized corporate services are worthless, or useless, or inefficiently rendered. Obviously there are values that can at times be attributed to bigness, and just as obviously there are well-run centralized corporations, just as there are sloppily run decentralized companies. The preceding examples and comments were admittedly exaggerated to drive home a point. But the reality cannot be denied that in the giant centralized organization in particular not all the services offered serve.

The Number One Fall Guy

Every fiasco in life has its fall guy. Or, as in this case, its great mass of fall guys. In the final analysis it is the public that is victimized by centralized management remotely administered. Centralized management fuels the fires of inflation as surely as if gasoline were poured on them.

It happens in a variety of ways. One example is the standardization that is a fetish with many large corporations. Purchasing, wages, fringe benefits, employment procedures, insurance—all are standardized to the hilt. In one corporation I know, job classifications fit into neat little slots regardless of what industry a division is in or where it is located. Thus a personnel manager is P-1, a credit manager is C-1, a produc-

tion manager is PR-1, and so on down the line. If a divisional
P-1 job calls for $22,000 a year, that's it nationwide. Of course,
there is some leeway, but not much. No attention is paid to
the reality that wages in one part of the country may be 20
percent lower than elsewhere. I have seen managers receive
automatic raises ranging from $3,000 to $10,000 on the heels
of having their companies taken over by a conglomerate. The
increase has to come from someplace, and is inevitably generated by boosting the selling price of the goods or services.

By the same token, I could cite more than one instance
where an ideally suited manager was turned down for a job
because, even though he was worth $28,000 per year, the cor-
porate table of organization called for $25,000. Again, it's the
public who pays if a second-rate manager is hired in place of
the one who would get better efficiency and a higher productivity yield from his people.

Another reason the public is the ultimate fall guy for the
large centralized corporation is that it is the nature of the 73rd-
floor occupants to stifle imagination and innovation. A classic
example is the book publishing business. During the past few
years most of the nation's independent book publishers have
been swallowed up by conglomerates. What this boils down
to in essence is that the editor's instinct and experience, developed over years of working with authors and books and observing the marketplace, are today discounted as virtually
meaningless in many publishing companies. Nowadays the final arbiter is the computer. If an editor loves a book and feels
it may be a living contribution to the literature or a particular
field of endeavor, the best he can hope for is an analytical run
through the computer to determine its market potential. If the
computer says O.K., there's a chance that the book may be
published. This effectively rules out new authors except in unusual cases, and it often rules out books that are considered
offbeat and where no track record exists for that particular category.

Great fiction, for example, can do much to save the world,
according to author Norman Mailer. How does he regard fiction today? "A basket case." Little wonder.

A related pet aversion of the large centralized corporation
is the introduction of new products. Unless the computer
printout states you can capture 10 percent of the market after

the first year, many companies won't lay out the investment capital needed. I know because I've been through this mill. It will cost, say, $5 million, to bring a new product from the drawing board into production and out to the market. Centralized corporate management wants this investment recouped in a hurry and a virtual guarantee that the new product will succeed. As any savvy businessperson knows, there's no such thing as a guarantee where new products are involved. The element of risk cannot be eliminated, computer printout or not. So the new product, however useful or promising it may appear to the divsion manager, never gets off the ground. And again, it's the public that pays.

D. G. Soergel, writing for *The Wall Street Journal,* states the case succinctly enough. "A national anti-enterprise policy is forcing would-be entrepreneurs to abandon plans for thousands of enterprises. It favors business expansions over new enterprises."* A key requirement of conglomerates is to recover capital costs in a hurry. Thus, says the writer, "the older and larger a firm becomes, the more it tends to concentrate on improving its product rather than inventing new ones." Improvement is beneficial, of course, It boosts efficiency and lowers costs. But it is detrimental as well. Innovation means progress, and one might argue the merits of improving products that should have been obsoleted and replaced years ago.

Another factor explaining the reluctance of large corporations to introduce new products is the "creative destruction of capital" aspect, as economists refer to it. New Products obsolete old products along with their tooling, design, and existing physical inventory, and it generally takes years to make up for the loss and generate profits on the new product line. Since the centralized corporation's favorite battle cry is "Bottom Line Now!" innovation runs counter to corporate objectives, and thus is suppressed.

* *The Wall Street Journal,* December 31, 1980.

CHAPTER 6

===

The Bondage Born of Bureaucracy

In an era of "future shock" and circumstances-triggered dynamism unprecedented in history, bureaucracy has become symbolic of staid and stubborn status-quoism. It stems from bigness and sameness, and most of all from centralized superstructurism. One would think the stifling paralysis evidenced time and again by bureaucracy in big government would serve as a lesson to business to steer clear of this route. But viewing the situation from a national vantage point, one cannot help but conclude that the message has been hammered across to a mere handful of thoughtful executives. One by one you can see the lumbering corporate giants, rendered inert by bureaucracy, stumble and falter and lose ground to the more innovative and imaginative decentralized minority. Indeed, far too much of U.S. government, commerce, and industry is being bottlenecked and dead-ended by a bondage born of bureaucracy.

How important is it for managers in all fields of enterprise to finger bureaucracy as the culprit it is? As important, I believe, as it is to protect and preserve America's free system and concept of personal and organizational independence and initiative. In fact, as history proves, bureaucratization and totalitarianism long have been bedfellows.

Italian sociologist Franco Ferrarotti sums it up in a nutshell. "Socialism might work if it were possible to invent a new

121

man, but until then capitalism has the advantage in inventiveness. The only thing that can kill capitalism is for it to slip into bureaucratic stagnation."*

In the same feature article, *Business Week* notes:

> Early capitalism did not foresee the rise and growth of the huge, bureaucratic corporation. Adam Smith opposed what he called the joint-stock company, arguing that hired managers would not work zealously for firms they did not own. More than a quarter-century ago, Harvard economist Joseph Schumpeter glumly concluded that the very success of capitalism would undermine it, as impersonal corporations grew up and swallowed the entrepreneurial spirit.

I can think of no greater challenge for the decades just ahead than that of initiating the aggressive action and restructuring so urgently needed to prevent this from happening.

The Devastating Effects of Bureaucracy

Levinson's Law of the Concrete Jungle states it simply enough: *Inefficiency multiplies in direct proportion to the organization's level of bureaucracy.*

It is a law that proves itself again and again. Inefficiency is a by-product of boredom. Boredom, states the management psychology newsletter *OBI Interaction,* "is the evil genius of the modern mass production system. Like Count Dracula, it hovers over office and factory, ready to sink its fangs into the unsuspecting employee."† It is the result of absolute predictability, the newsletter goes on to say. Commitment and involvement are the result of uncertainty about *possible* achievement. Part of the contemporary problem is that precision machinery has removed much of the uncertainty about the outcome of work.

In my personal experience, the most devastating kind of precision machine is the headquarters-based, computer-bred numerologist. His impact is to depersonalize work and initiative at all levels of supervision and management. He is the ultimate creator of boredom. As the psychologists point out, "achievement is real only if it includes some element of

---

*Business Week, April 21, 1980.
†February 1, 1978.

uniqueness that can be identified with the individual." To the computer-bred numerologist, "uniqueness" is a dirty word.

There are several ways to escape being bored: (1) listen to everyone you meet, (2) make sure that your job challenges your powers, and (3) keep your mind alive.

Any thoughtful person who was exposed first-hand to the paralyzing effects of impersonal remote-control management can relate these points to the centralized status-quorocracy.

1. One of the most difficult and frustrating tasks of the remotely controlled divisional manager is that of simply getting himself listened to—really listened to—by the headquarters powers that be.

2. In far too many cases the only real challenge confronting the divisional executive of the centralized corporation is that of successfully sidestepping the multiplicity of strictures imposed upon him.

3. Bureaucracy deadens the mind as well as the spirit. The only functions the divisional executive is permitted to do for himself are the ones he is instructed by Big Daddy to perform, and in the time and manner prescribed.

Deadly boredom, as you can see, is an automatic by-product of bureaucracy, which, in turn, is a by-product of centralized management in nine out of ten cases.

MANAGERS AND MISMANAGERS

The obedient, well-behaved, "ideal" manager in the centralized superstructure, who gets a good-boy pat on the head from Big Daddy, is characterized as a "mismanager" by one astute observer of the modern business scene, Ichak Adizes. He writes, "This manager acts exclusively as an administrator. He is a manager who knows by heart the standard operating procedures in the organization and manages by means of directives that are usually presented in writing."*

They are not *all* presented in writing, of course. One of the unwritten directives from headquarters is, "Hey, buddy, don't think for yourself; that's what we're here for." To violate this unspoken mandate is to incur Big Daddy's wrath. I speak from personal experience. As a violator I incurred it, and today am out on my ear—to my immense and grateful relief.

* "Mismanagement Styles," *California Management Review,* Winter 1976, p. 5.

Standard operating procedures (SOP), as Adizes points out, constitute the slowly beating heart of bureaucratic mismanagement. The more centrally controlled the structure, the more rigidly documented and prescribed the procedures. The obedient, well-behaved mismanager, in time rendered mindless by the system, has as his Bible the Corporate Policy Manual with its supporting concordance, the Procedural Text.

Every function is standardized and homogenized to the hilt. The "Bible" tells you how to act with and react to customers, how to compensate and treat personnel, how to respond to labor problems and issues. Where deviations occur, the Good Book states, do nothing, do not pass GO, do not collect $200. Instead, sound the alarm. Big Daddy will be there when you need Him.

One trouble with superstandardization, especially where it affects and involves people, is that human beings do not fit standard molds. Every person is different, every individual unique. Any experienced line manager worth his salt will tell you that you can't treat every employee, every supplier, every customer the same. You have to tailor your approach to the individual's special needs, motivations, temperament, and quirks.

Out of my own experience I can call to mind one employee whose primary need was security. He was bright and competent, but in taking over a new assignment it was important for him to feel comfortable with it, unthreatened. He liked you to spell out the procedure every step of the way, to provide maximum assurance he would be able to handle the job to your satisfaction. Another employee I can recall, given the same assignment, would be impatient if you spelled it out for him in too much detail. He looked upon each new task as a challenge, evaluated it in terms of the career opportunity it presented. A third employee was well equipped in terms of experience, training, and intelligence to handle almost any task you assigned to him—provided he could do the job on his own and didn't have to work with other people.

The great centrobureaucracy doesn't allow for human differences and individual needs. People are numbered, assignments are numbered, and if Person 3642 is given Job 146, there's nothing more to discuss or consider. Just as the computer doesn't differentiate between characteristics and temperament, its progeny, the numerologists, proceed on the premise that employees, customers, suppliers, consumers are all formed from mass-produced molds. Ironically, the huge international conglomerate, in this respect at least, is all too often alarmingly like the depersonalized communist behemoth it professes to despise with such venom.

POWER POLITICS

Bottom-line objectives and the goals of self-aggrandizement that inspire power politics in bureaucratic environments are about as compatible as actress Jane Fonda and the Moral Majority's Jerry Falwell. In one miniconglomerate, the overstaffed headquarters office was like a battleground, with six armies participating in the conflict. In disjointed control were six "generals," all vying for power and eventual succession to the presidency. Fortunes were made or blown on subordinates' choice of enlistment. As one former manager stated the case: "Line up with the right faction, and you'll get a good crack at a better job and a fat year-end bonus. Select the wrong horse, and you're most likely dead-ended."

Not surprisingly, remarks pro or critical always seemed to get wide circulation, so that it became a matter of winning the favor of the general of your choice without unduly antagonizing others, a delicate juggling act. Managers were so strongly involved in the power play that decisions and priorities were based not on what was good for the organization but on speculation regarding the personal consequences. Ultimately a management consultant was hired in an effort to restore some semblance of order and direction to the company. In describing the situation to me, the consultant confided that in his personal file he referred to the headquarters group as "Operation Brownnose."

One consequence of internecine warfare of this kind is that it turns off the competent manager who believes in performance as the sole criterion for personal advancement and growth. There's nothing like the centrobureaucracy to whet a good manager's appetite for a small, tightly knit operation. If you are seeking personal independence and control over your own destiny, your chances of getting it rise in proportion to the operation's sense of purpose and direction and its leanness.

What's more, states an industrial psychologist, you are also more aware of your own value and contribution, and the simple human side is more fun.

It's Time to Take a Cue from Big Government

In his book *Revolt of the Haves,** Robert Kuttner laments the inefficiency of bureaucratic big government. He cites numerous so called social reforms in America that have failed due to too many cooks making too many studies with the result of too many decisions made by too many "experts" far removed from the scene.

The bigger big government gets, the more inefficient it becomes. Clearly, big government in America is bigger than big government in West Germany. Kuttner points out the intriguing fact tht 20 percent of the U.S. work force is in government, while in Germany, which spends 20 percent more proportionally on the public sector, government employees account for only 15 percent.

Indeed, a *Time* special report notes that "when the Constitution makers devised their system of checks and balances, they had no idea that a gigantic federal bureaucracy would some day check everything and balance very little."† The report goes on to explain that the bureaucracy today numbers 2.8 million people, almost all of whom are protected by the civil service, so no president can really make them do what he wants. "Merit" raises, it concludes, went to 99 percent of the bureaucrats last year, and practically nobody got dismissed for incompetence, a procedure that until recently took anywhere up to two years of appeals at an average cost to the taxpayers of $100,000 per appeal.

While it is true that a great many more heads are axed each year in business than in government—often irrationally, or as a result of power play and political pussyfooting—I could reel off a long list of internationally known corporate giants whose centrobureaucracies rival those of big government.

In my opinion, if every U.S. chief executive whose company is centralized were to sit down with an open mind, ponder the following questions with his own organization in mind,

*New York: Simon & Schuster, 1980.
†"American Renewal," *Time*, February 23, 1981, p. 44.

respond to them objectively and, where needed, take the corrective action indicated, this nation's productivity would shoot up 30 percent in a hurry.

1. Running down major corporate functions one at a time: "Do we really need 22 or 28 headquarters people in marketing; 19 or 23 people in purchasing; 14 or 17 people in personnel; 86 people in data processing—or whatever the function or number happens to be?

2. Is the superstandardization achieved in personnel policies, purchasing, labor relations, compensation, sales, advertising, and so on practical from the perspective of the division management team in Oshkosh, Twin Forks, San Diego, and Bangor, Maine? Is its effect to enhance or to detract from bottom-line performance?

3. Are the headquarters "experts" who are making decisions and handing down mandates for the division people to enforce really better qualified and better informed regarding the facility's problems and needs than the managers employed there? Could they conceivably be as sensitive and (from a human standpoint) as responsive to the individual needs and motivations of division personnel?

4. Are the top division people competent to solve important problems and make decisions on their own in such areas of operation as marketing, personnel, labor relations, manufacturing, and research? If the answer is no, would it make sense to upgrade divisional skills or staff the operation with higher-level people who could be trained to do the job on an on-hand basis?

5. How many programs and projects exist at corporate headquarters, in the divisions, or anywhere else in the organization that have long ago outlived their usefulness, were never beneficial to profits to begin with, and should have been discontinued months or years ago?

If you examine each one of these items, you will quickly note the extent to which the problem capsulized applies to big government at its worst. Every president who ever took office, from John Adams to Ronald Reagan, conceded that excessive layerism was present in government and vowed to scalp waste from the system. Anyone who ever filled out a tax return or federal or state "Information Request" could discuss at length and profanely the evils of superstandardization. Decisions? Remotely based government "experts" decide issues ad infinitum, ranging from the number of students in Harlem classrooms to the design of wallboard partitions in West Virginia plants. Programs? The *Time* article cites a classic example: the Rural Electrification Administration was set up in 1935 as an emergency relief program to bring electricity to the American farm. Today more than 99 percent of farms are electrified, but the REA still has 740 people spending a budget of $29 million. If a directory of obsolete federal programs, many of them unbelievably useless in today's economy, were compiled, it would probably take more pages than "Gone with the Wind."

Isn't it time for Big Business to take a cue from Big Government?

Standardized Salesmanship

One of the most ruinous impacts of bureaucratization is that the individual is lost sight of—not only those people employed at corporate divisions and branches, but the ones with whom they do business as well. Practically, realistically, psychologically, and any other way you could name, there is a great deal of difference between the way we act and react when we confront the people with whom we do business face to face and the way we respond when those people are faceless, nothing more than numbers or factors.

Selling is particularly significant in this regard. I could cite innumerable situations where centralized standardization— spelling out and rigidly prescribing in headquarters policy manuals and directives how to deal with customers and respond to requests and complaints under varying circumstances—antagonized buyers and sent them scurrying, to the delight of competitors. People are created as individuals and become increasingly individualistic and independent as they grow in stature and status.

In my experience, this is at least as true, if not more true, of people who buy and sell goods than of most others in business. The sales representative who, on his own much of the time, must use his own judgment, make his own decisions, and, in large measure, plan his own strategies, is in a very real sense an entrepreneur even though he's employed. His personality, style, selling instinct, and savvy play important roles in determining the way customers respond and the amount of business he does. Since this is a factor that cannot be computerized, the marketing experts at headquarters very often ignore it.

Here are some case histories that dramatize the consequences of standardized salesmanship by the book instead of the person.

A dynamic and personable rep in the stationery and forms industry earned customer appreciation and loyalty through his determination to make life as easy and problem-free as he could for the buyer. Taking one key customer as an example, the buyer and salesman had over the years developed a friendly personal relationship. The buyer relied on the rep to keep track of his inventory for him and, if he happened to need a particular form in a hurry, to get it for him within 24 hours. The rep did this mainly through his own devices. He had his own virtually foolproof inventory system. He also kept a small stockpile of standard forms in his basement so that he could get to them fast in an emergency. These strategies had paid off for years. Then one day the forms company was acquired. Enter Big Daddy and standardization.

Big Daddy had a big computer, which had a high-speed inventory system programmed into it. Theory: the computer could read out any customer's inventory status within microseconds; this relieved the sales rep of inventory-keeping chores, thus releasing his precious selling time for more direct customer contacts. Unfortunately, the system worked well only in theory. It couldn't match the personal attention and reliability of the rep's home-grown system. Moreover, salespeople keeping their own supply of forms in their homes could lead to all sorts of complications and shenanigans, according to Dad. The practice was henceforth condemned.

You guessed the outcome. Friendship for the rep or not, deprived of two long-accustomed services that had become important to him, the customer deserted and now deals with a competitor.

Another case occurred five years ago in the furniture industry. The division manager and his key marketing team were summoned to their recently adopted parent's Philadelphia-based headquarters for an important "policy and indoctrination" meeting. Here the law was laid down to them.

A study had been conducted and a computer-based conclusion drawn that division profitability could be increased 30 percent within two years. How? A series of rules and strictures was spelled out. One called for the immediate elimination of unprofitable and marginal accounts.

On paper this made all the sense in the world. In the field it did not. The mandate was for sales management to review with each salesperson his roster of customers. Accounts were to survive or be dropped in accordance with a rigidly prescribed set of standards as determined by computer-based marketing criteria. One sales rep affected was Alice, and one customer affected was Davidson Brothers (not their real names). According to the standards spelled out in Big Daddy's directive, Davidson Brothers was on the hit list.

"This is a mistake," Alice argued. "While it's true that Davidson shows up as marginal on the computer printouts, the company's potential is good. A sharp and savvy manager took over the business six months ago, and the outlook is excellent. I couldn't prove my case with statistics, but based on my experience in the field, I have faith in this customer. I wouldn't advise dropping him."

"Experience in the field"? No such factor existed in the computer's analysis. As you predicted, Alice lost out. Today Davidson Brothers is a growing key account in the area—being served by one of the company's most formidable competitors.

I believe that in most cases headquarters-based executives, removed from the actual transacting of business, fail to appreciate the value of such things as salesmanship and the importance of personal service. It's not that they lack understanding or intelligence. Their world of numbers simply excludes the human factor. They aren't accustomed to dealing with it.

The Right to Know

A cherished American right, diligently espoused by both the press and communicators in government, is the citizen's right to be kept informed regarding issues and matters concerning him. But, as an unemployed mother of 14 children whose husband deserted her might tell you, even motherhood can be overdone.

The great majority of executives employed in the head-quarters of large centralized conglomerates would confirm that the right-to-know concept is too often as overdone as a 12-minute steak left on the burner an hour. I've seen it time and again. Everybody who is anybody in the central office has to know what's going on. Not only does he want to know what happened recently; he also wants to know what is likely to happen. If you know, you're "with it." If you don't, you're left out.

I asked one such manager the other day, "How much time would you say you spend getting information or giving information to others? Include the time you take to read memos, reports, and other written materials."

He thought a few moments, then said, shaking his head, "It's an almost impossible question to answer. It never stops. It goes on all the time."

When I pinned him down, he admitted there were days when he spent four hours or more on information one way or another. His title was product development manager.

When I was at American Standard, at certain times of the month in particular, the telephones rang incessantly: How do the figures look? Do you think we'll hit 40,000 on Product X this month? Will we beat last month's sales? When planning and budget time rolls around, a new round of questions are asked: How does it look? How are we doing? I don't have the latest figures, ask Harry. He doesn't know. Well, call Bill. It goes on and on like a broken record—and that's just the calls.

When it comes to memos and reports, information that's produced in triplicate in the decentralized company is expanded, not only from the standpoint of data content, but in the number of copies produced. Executives number 6, 7, 8, 9, 10, 11, and 12 on the distribution list may merely glance at the report, or not look at it at all. But in the centralized company you're either included or left out. And if you're left out, from the political standpoint you are somehow diminished.

I couldn't tell you how many times I've heard the question

posed in an annoyed and indignant tone of voice: "Why isn't my name on the list to receive this report?" No one would ever think to reply: "Because you don't need it, dummy!"

Other truckloads of information are generated because managers feel they need to protect or cover themselves. If something happens—an error, misjudgment, or conflict—and it bounces back to you, if you have a memo or report you can allude to, you're safe. "Check out paragraph three of the memo I sent you March 15th, where I said that it might be a problem." Or, "I made that point in my report of April 3rd, but you didn't do anything about it."

I've got a suggestion to make to the chief executive officer of every heavily centralized company: decentralize. If you won't decentralize, buy a paper company. Every centralized corporation should own a paper company. It would save the stockholders money.

The Waste of Human Resources

The most tragic and costly corporate waste of all is the waste of human resources. The more centralized the organization, the larger and more unwieldy its structure, the more likely it is that this will occur. The most obvious people-related profit drainage stems from layered management hierarchies and their personnel excesses. But this is only one way to waste human resources.

WORK UNRELATED TO PROFIT OBJECTIVES

Starting in the 1960s and carried through to the 1970s and 1980s, the trend toward computer-based planning and research developed into a race among large corporations to determine who could come up fastest with the greatest amount of sophisticated and esoteric gimmickry. One company, Caterpillar Tractor Co., is notable in that it consistently ignored these techniques and based its philosophy on the long-established basics of business. As a reward, in an industry hard hit by recession and retrenchment, Caterpillar's sales volume increased during periods when its major competitors, International Harvester, Deere, Clark Equipment, and JI Case, all suffered earnings declines.

The economy is starting to get the message, according to a

Business Week feature story. "Leading universities are again emphasizing operations courses, and companies are again promoting executives with broad-based rather than specialized skills. A back-to-basics movement is taking hold, with practices that Caterpillar has always used."*

When research becomes esoteric to the point of confusion, it sometimes becomes an end in itself independent of profit objectives. I know one marketing manager employed by a giant food corporation who reached this conclusion years ago. "But if I'd pooh-poohed the far-out surveys and research too adamantly," he told me, "I would have been blasted out of my job by the numbers-happy chart readers. So I went along in self-defense."

He recalled one occasion where a task force of Harvard-bred whiz kids dreamed up a computer survey to determine what the public would like in the way of desserts. He regarded the study as worthless and implied as much to the liaison man from the consulting firm that had been paid a fat fee to conduct it.

"If you feel that way," said the researcher, "why did you order it?"

"Because it appeases the top brass. They like to see their investment supported by statistical evidence of its wisdom. You show me the slide-rule or computer technique that can top the good old-fashioned practice of questioning users to find out how the damned product tastes, and I'll retire and learn how to clip coupons."

The man from the survey firm left him his copies of the charts, matrixes and reports. My friend shoved them into a file and never gave them a second look.

DUPLICATION

Market planning is a good function to use in pinpointing corporate waste. Each division has a planning department. Every year it fills out a bundle of forms specifying projected market potential, what its share ought to be, strategies devised to meet its objectives, and the capital outlay it will need. By the time all the forms are completed, explanations are made, and evidence is documented, a fat book is created. The book

---

*May 4, 1981.

goes to group headquarters. There group market planners review and redo all the data. This becomes part of a total marketing plan. One plan I can recall encompasses five divisions in all and is gargantuan.

The overall plan, together with other overall plans submitted by group planning units, now goes to corporate headquarters for presentation to the president. But before it reaches the top-executive suite, the group plans must be consolidated and reviewed again by the corporate market planning department. An inflation rate must be calculated and pertinent economic factors—housing starts, area unemployment, interest rates, and so on—added to the mix.

Throughout this procedure there are continuing input and feedback at all levels. If the division doesn't agree with the group assessment on any one of dozens of items, as is always the case, explanations must be made, alternatives suggested. Same thing all down the line. This entails additional studies and research. In the end, the division people know they can't win, because Big Daddy is even tougher to fight than City Hall. But the amount of time, work, and manpower that goes into the procedure keeps growing and growing, much of it duplicating and rehashing tasks that are done over and over again.

The windup is that if you're in the division, you accept group or headquarters figures and decisions you don't believe in. And you cheat, lie, and falsify to a degree Pinocchio never would have dreamed of doing, to win as many points as you can.

MEETINGS THAT DON'T MEET OBJECTIVES

I think I've discovered the fastest and most efficient way to kill time and ruin productivity: appoint a useless committee and sit it down to an unnecessary meeting. Sound bright? It's done all the time in the overpeopled centralized organization, where responsibility dodging is an ancient and revered practice.

In my opinion, if every executive who planned a meeting were required to present two specific statements up front—(1) What is this meeting's objective? (2) How much does it cost?—75 percent of all meetings would be eliminated. Among other findings, a recent survey revealed that 54 percent of the man-

agers queried felt inessential meetings were held in their organizations; about half thought that even useful meetings were
too long, and a whopping 76 percent admitted they lacked
sufficient time for creative thinking and planning activities.

My experience bears this out. Some meetings are valuable.
When you want to bring a number of minds or disciplines to
bear on an idea or problem, it is often an ideal form of communication. For a meeting to be productive, it must start
promptly at a prespecified time and end at a prespecified time
or sooner. When I ran Steelcraft Manufacturing Co., a favorite
strategy of mine was to conduct ad hoc stand-up meetings to
make sure that this happened. It's astounding how much time
can be wasted when people are settled comfortably around a
conference table.

The most wasteful of all meetings, especially prevalent in
the centralized multidivisional corporation, is the one where
divisional representatives are summoned to attend. I have seen
heads of divisions and their top aides flown to New York City
from such points as Cincinnati, Dallas, and Seattle for a 30-
minute meeting and then flown back.

Out of curiosity I costed out one meeting that could have
been conducted as effectively over the telephone and, when
you really got down to it, could have been dispensed with
entirely. Its purpose was to familiarize divisional managers with
a planning procedure corporate headquarters wished to standardize throughout the organization. No opinions were expressed, no ideas thrown out and evaluated, no multidisciplined thinking brought to bear on a problem. The meeting
was purely instructional. A 30-page written procedure would
have served the purpose as well. I won't even discuss the pros
and cons of the purpose itself. But 44 people were flown into
New York, fed and sheltered in a fine New York hotel, and
flown home the next day.

Since I am now in the hotel business I have become a strong
advocate of this practice. I think a great many such meetings
should be held, preferably in the sunny state of Florida. Can
you blame me? The particular meeting in question, including
executive time, travel expense, and hotel bills, costed out in
excess of $50,000.

It has been my experience that the more divisions a corporation has, the more departments set up at corporate head-

quarters, the more department heads, assistants, and assistant assistants it employs, the more meetings it tends to hold and the more the cost soars. It has also been my experience that half the meetings announced are held to lay down the law. Here's how Big Daddy wants the procurement process to take place. He wants it done this way and that way and this way. Holding a meeting to exchange ideas is one thing, holding it to spell out procedures quite another.

Another thing about meetings in the centralized corporation: more often than not, even when you have an idea to put forth, or an alternative solution to propose, you're not permitted to do it. The reason's quite simple and inviolable in the name of "efficiency": the "deviation" was not on the agenda.

The Most Common Time Wasters

How is time most commonly wasted in the bureaucratic environment? The following checklist spells out the most prevalent examples.

Meetings. Extended and/or unessential.

Communication. Memos, directives, reports—extensive and superfluous—with excessive distributions. The infinite detail generated by bureaucracies, and the endless telephone calls required to attend to the detail.

Studies and surveys. Prepared by committees, task forces, individual employees, and hired consultants.

Extended lunch hours. Often in the guise of informal meetings.

Travel. Usually to and from meetings.

Interruptions. Interruptions, and more interruptions.

Campaigning. In response to the political climate that exists in every bureaucracy.

Regulations. The larger the bureaucracy, the greater the money involved, the more closely it is monitored by the largest bureaucracy of all, the government, and the more forms and reports it is required to file.

Retraining. The larger the bureaucracy, the greater the level of human frustration, the more extensive the turnover—hence the training and retraining requirements expand in proportion to the in-and-out manpower flow.

I recently talked with a plant manager who quit a $95,000-a-year job with a large corporation to accept a similar position for $20,000 a year less with a company one-fifth the size. The reason: "I was consistently working 12-hour days. I spent seven hours on my regular necessary work, five hours a day on all the crap that was generated as a result of the bureaucracy. It got to me after a while."

The Perpetuation of Deadwood

The care and feeding of corporate deadwood and dry rot should be no different from the care and feeding of deadwood and dry rot in your garden. You prune it, clip it, and cart it away. In the centralized corporation, however, the deadwood is permitted to persist and choke out the organization's healthy and normal growth.

Business author Raymond Dreyfack writes in his book *Sure Fail—The Art of Mismanagement:* "How does bureaucracy breed incompetence? The answer is simple enough—the system feeds on itself. Typically the new organization starts off lean, tight, and purposeful. But as it grows in size, the work spreads out. Key personnel hire aides, and the aides hire aides. The layers multiply and flourish."*

The centralized bureaucracy is at a further disadvantage because of the frustration level the structure tends to produce. Typically, the talented and self-confident managers get the message quickly enough and seek less strictured pastures. The ne'er-do-wells, marginal employees, and staffers with personality problems, insecure and uncomfortable with themselves, cling to their jobs, happy to have found a place where they are tolerated.

I have seen it happen time and again in the centralized environment. Managers pervert Andrew Carnegie's famous counsel and paraphrase it to read: "The smart manager is the one who knows how to surround himself with subordinates *less* able than he is."

The rationale is as simple as it is detrimental to profit goals. The less capable your aides and associates, the smarter you

* New York: Morrow, 1976, p. 83.

look. Only in a genuine bureaucracy could this philosophy prevail. Its natural by-product is waste and incompetence, creating the worst kind of profit drainage.

Writes Dreyfack: "Too often a manager's status is measured more by his personal sphere of influence than by the job that he does."

One example of this took place in the computer center of a large centralized California conglomerate. It was a typical environment where the numbers jugglers, narrow short-term planners, and chartists reigned supreme. Not surprisingly, the cagey EDP man who over a seven-year period had elevated himself from data processing manager to vice president of information and communications, was the ruling faction's fair-haired boy.

He systematically built his staff from 53 to 138 people and more than tripled his salary. Deadwood in this company was nurtured and cultivated with loving care instead of zapped as soon as it was found inadequate and failing to contribute to profit objectives. Eventually, when, despite increasing sales in most major divisions, earnings wavered and shrank, a consulting firm was called in on the board's insistence to learn why. For one thing, it found, the long-exalted information and communications VP had been making every effort he could to fulfill any and all corporate requests for more computer printouts and reports, whether they were needed or not. For another thing, the consultants compared the size of the corporation's data processing operation with that of competitors and, in some cases, found it double the size. Their recommendation was to chop the department in half. A complete "reorganization" was required to cut the deadwood out of the system and achieve this objective.

Ichak Adizes of the Graduate School of Management, University of California, Los Angeles, notes that the deadwood bureaucrat is apathetic:

> He waits to be told what to do. He does not produce; he does not administer others zealously; he does not worry about power intrigues; and obviously he does not provide sparks. . . . If he has any "sparking" ideas, he keeps them to himself. He is mostly worried about how to survive until retirement and how to keep intact the little he has. In his ample free time

138

he looks for successes that he can take the credit for, a strategy intended to improve his chances of survival.*

Most of all, the deadwood survivor, however technically or administratively ineffective he may be, is an ace politician. He is usually amiable and likable. At one practice he's an expert: he knows whose boots to lick. He is often a political whiz. Deadwood cannot survive in the efficiently managed decentralized operation where status, promotion, and compensation are based on continually monitored and evaluated performance with prestated organizational objectives in mind. Here profit contribution is the criterion. The individual either achieves reasonable and realistic standards, or does not, and is rewarded accordingly.

The well-run decentralized company features fulfillment and growth. The bureaucracy winds up facing an increasingly problematic profit drain.

*"Mismanagement Styles," *California Management Review,* Winter 1976.

PART III

Radical Decentralization: How to Do It

CHAPTER 7

=============

Decentralizing the Operation

A Conference Board report* defines decentralization as the delegation of decision-making authority to lower (or remote) levels of the organization. It pinpoints three factors that have a major effect on this process:

1. The confidence factor—the degree of confidence of superiors in the competence of subordinates.
2. The information factor—the extent to which information is fed to the decision-making points, and the feedback system that permits superiors to evaluate decision results.
3. The scope-of-impact factor—the extent to which decisions made in one unit affect the operation of another unit.

It is my contention that the benefits of radical decentralization described in this book are applicable in any organizational unit or division where qualified executives are employed, communications inadequacies do not hamper operations, and the operations of the unit and other units are not interdependent.

Seven Keys to Radical Decentralization—Overview

What are the main considerations in establishing a radically decentralized company—or operation and defining its parameters? Here are seven keys:

* "On Concepts of Corporate Structure," *Conference Board Record,* February 1974.

Key No. 1: The divisions or sections of the decentralized unit must be defined. If it is to break down into ten pieces, each piece must be spelled out. Thus, if all ten pieces are related to the furniture industry, divisional autonomy would not extend to the division president's freedom to start a gambling casino or car rental agency as piece number 11.

Key No. 2: The unit's continuity, direction, and homogeneity must be decided and agreed upon in advance so that managers are well aware of limitations applicable to ventures and other business opportunities. If exceptions are made, they would be with corporate approval only.

Key No. 3: Leadership must be defined and scope of leadership clearly established. Before a unit can be successfully decentralized, any and all doubt must be removed right down the line regarding the capability of the unit president and subordinate managers to run the main show and side shows confidently and competently.

Key No. 4: The purpose of the business must be defined, its major goals and subgoals enumerated. What is this operation going to do for the corporation and the world? What will be its role in the industry and the community? These questions must be answered before decentralized management can be initiated.

Key No. 5: The ground rules for radical decentralization must be established. How will the unit's master plan and budget be developed? By whom, and by when? Are enough staff and talent on hand to set up a strategic operating plan including balance sheet, income statement, capital-expenditure plans, and cash-flow forecasts, along with defining other business and financial requirements? This must all be determined in advance.

Key No. 6: Corporate headquarters must set up the ground rules under which the unit's master plan will operate. Return on investment and acceptable profit margins must be spelled out and perceived by unit managers as reasonable and realistic. How much money will be earmarked by the corporation for capital investment, how much plowed back into the unit each year?

Key No. 7: Finally, corporate headquarters will have to establish checkpoints for monitoring and measuring the unit's success periodically. Will this be done weekly, monthly, yearly? What deviations are and are not acceptable?

In a nutshell, these are the seven keys. But the master key superimposed on all seven is *the people you work with*. Decentralization isn't a success formula; the only insurance it provides is that managers will be left alone to manage. The *quality* of management is always the main deciding factor so far as results are concerned—profit versus loss, success versus failure. In the radically decentralized environment, savvy and competent leadership is an absolute essential; there is no "other guy" upon whom to depend.

WHO IS AT THE END OF THE LEASH?

Key No. 4 specifies the importance of defining the operation's purpose and goals. It goes without saying that the personal goals of division executives must be compatible with divisional—and overall corporate—goals for the enterprise to succeed. "Right now," states *The New York Times* writer Daniel F. Cuff, "the lid is popping off at American Can. After years of comfortable profits, earnings plummeted 33 percent last year [1980]."*

There is little question that the "Sam Goody affair," in which a Brooklyn Federal Court found the American Can subsidary guilty of dealing in thousands of counterfeit tapes of popular music, is responsible for a substantial amount of the lid popping. The embarrassing, image-soiling experience is unquestionably causing the conglomerate's chairman William Woodside, president Frank Connor, and other top brass at its Connecticut headquarters some hard soul-searching and re-evaluation that encompass all its divisions. In what has been termed a "fundamental redirection," at last report the company wants to spin off no less than 25 percent of its far-flung operations.

At least one analyst, Cuff reports, sees a significant cause of American Can's current problems and shrinking margins in headquarters' permissiveness in allowing division managers— and especially managers at the Sam Goody unit—"to operate on too long a leash." (key No. 7) It has been my experience

---

* *The New York Times,* April 19, 1981.

145

that where competent, proven, and well-intentioned managers are in control, the longer the leash, the better. But where the leash is long, the bulldog at the other end better be tough, resolute, and capable of making the most of whatever bones are available.

A Target to Shoot For

A recent McKinsey & Co. study* of management practices in 37 companies selected as models of managerial effectiveness concluded that these organizations had eight common attributes:

1. A bias toward action.
2. Simple form and lean staff.
3. Continued contact with customers.
4. Productivity improvement through people.
5. Operational automomy to encourage entrepreneurship.
6. Stress on one key business value.
7. Emphasis on doing what they know best.
8. Simultaneous loose and tight controls.

Examine the traits closely. They constitute a virtual definition of the radically decentralized company. While these 37 organizations employ modern management tools, the study made clear they do not rely on such techniques as management by objectives, operations research, or zero-base budgeting to succeed. The computer is used as a tool, nothing more. It is neither a pilot nor an architect that dictates and designs corporate strategy.

As specific steps in decentralizing and humanizing the organization are discussed in these four chapters, you may find it useful to turn back to this model to see how those steps contribute to the goal of managerial effectiveness.

Evaluating the Status Quo

The first step in the decentralization effort is to assess just how far the organization is removed from the ideal—the flex-

Business Week, July 21, 1980.

ible, fast-moving, radically decentralized company, imbued with entrepreneurial spirit and respect for people and their needs. Here is a list of issues that should be addressed.

- *Evaluate action mobility.* How fast do your company's key people move when there's an important problem to solve or decision to make? How many reporting levels and approvals are required before an action can be finalized?
- *Assess corporate risk-taking frequency.* When tough decisions are on the boards, are they often bogged down in committees? Are managers more often than not determined to play it safe rather than stick out their necks, even if they're convinced they are right?
- *Check managerial meddling.* How much freedom of action do division executives get? Do they speak their minds openly? Are they too often thwarted and frustrated so far as work goals are concerned? Is it a major production to get headquarters approval for a suggested innovation or change?
- *Test the entrepreneurial climate.* Are divisional—and head-quarters—entrepreneurial types encouraged or discouraged? How tough a task is it to convince top management it's worthwhile departing from the beaten path where a lot of money is involved? Are radical new ideas frowned upon or greeted with interest? Is it economically advantageous for a young comer to give his imagination and ambition full rein?
- *Find out who does the planning.* Is the drawing up of division plans and guidelines an exercise in futility? Do they merely serve as a conversational base to be torn to shreds and revised drastically by headquarters planners, with little justification you can see for major changes and denials?
- *Examine new-venture financing.* Is headquarters top brass rigid regarding divisional venture proposals? Is the division required to stick very close to its knitting? Have you seen potential money-making venture ideas within your company's field of expertise sloshed down the drain because Big Daddy was too slow or reluctant to part with the bucks needed for action to take place?
- *Inspect morale under a microscope.* Are supervisors, middle managers, and high-level managers gung ho for the corporation? Do they feel they can grow and develop in the organization if they prove their ability to their superiors? Or do they

feel dead-ended and jaded, as if they were banging their heads against a relentless stone wall?

• *Check out the political climate.* Are advancement and the achievement of individual career objectives more dependent on whom you know and how you kowtow to them than on the level of performance you display? If a manager is outstanding in his field, are his chances of recognition and promotion good regardless of his political affiliations and loyalties? Which pays off best: doing a praiseworthy job or making the most strategic connections?

• *Evaluate levels of compensation.* Are key managers well paid? Do they get more or less money and perks than the industry average? If managerial pay scales are low, is this because little managerial skill is required, since most important decisions and problems are handled from headquarters?

In the radically decentralized company, again assuming a competent management team, all these factors, from action mobility to compensation levels, would be found to be adequate. In the centralized organization, many of them will be in urgent need of improvement.

Preparing the Way

As I said earlier in this chapter, savvy and competent leadership is absolutely essential in the radically decentralized organization, even more so than under centralization. Why? Because managers in the divisions cannot rely on remote-control bosses at headquarters to make the final decisions for them.

This point has been made bluntly and harshly time and again in the real world of the marketplace. Notes a recent *Business Week* Management Report: "Decentralization, when it works, provides some clear benefits to a company," and goes on to enumerate them. But, the report continues, "decentralization can lead to disaster when the chief—as well as some divisional managers—are weak. That is how many observers describe the fragmented Public Broadcasting Service (PBS)."*

The article portrays PBS as an organization under siege and wonders if it can survive without a strong management team. Local stations, given autonomy, look to PBS, not for leader-

---

* "Public Broadcasting's Trouble at the Top," *Business Week,* March 9, 1981, p. 104.

ship but for integration of program delivery, according to some frustrated insiders. Missing are overall direction from headquarters and accountability to the parent for results, a clear violation of keys No. 3, 6, and 7 discussed at the beginning of this chapter. Managers are selected locally, the Management Report points out, and answer only to their boards of governors rather than to PBS chief executive Lawrence K. Grossman.

On top of that, some critics charge that the network has lost sight of its goals (key No. 4), the main one being to fulfill informational and cultural needs bypassed by commercial programming. Sharp contrast is drawn with its less affluent cousin, National Public Radio, which gets less than a sixth of the total public-broadcasting funding but has won high marks for its performance. Much of the credit goes to journalist Frank Mankiewicz, a former Robert Kennedy aide, for his management talent and strong leadership qualities.

Another decentralized victim of alleged weak management is, or was, Swiss-headquartered Nestlé Co.'s U.S. and Canadian enterprise. U.S. Nestlé's growth performance to date has fallen far short of target, and the company is being outstripped by competitors. The American operation is currently being restructured under U.S.-born David E. Guerrant, who came to Nestlé from Libby in the 1960s, where he is credited with turning the then ailing company into a winner.

Guerrant attributes much of the U.S. operation's trouble to its former autonomy. Here management weakness resulted not from lack of competence but misfortune. Eleven Nestlé managers died in a Stouffer Inn fire in Harrison, NY, six from the coffee division alone, which was already engaged in a fierce competitive battle with General Foods and Procter & Gamble.

Misfortune or not, there is no substitute for strong leadership and knowledgeable decision making (keys No. 3 and 5). It is thus no surprise that control at Nestlé under Guerrant, a highly qualified executive with a proven track record, is now being centralized. Notes one Wall Street observer: "The best thing Dave Guerrant could do at this point is to develop strong management teams in the divisions, then decentralize again from a position of strength."*

* *Business Week,* February 2, 1981.

STRENGTHENING LOCAL MANAGEMENT

If local management is weak, proceeding with full-scale decentralization is unlikely to produce favorable results. The first goal must be to upgrade the quality of local management. To put it another way, radical decentralization depends on the complete faith of corporate top management in the local management teams—but that faith cannot be blind, it must be based on merit.

What specific actions can corporate top management take to develop stronger local management teams in preparation for decentralization? Here are some suggestions.

Identify and replace weak incumbents. Starting from the top, eliminate incompetent (or move misplaced) managers.

Don't hesitate to add line positions where this would strengthen the operation. Wield the ax at the headquarters staff, not the troops on the firing line. As an example, when B. Charles Ames took over as chief executive of Acme-Cleveland Corp. in 1980, he eliminated a large number of corporate staff positions, but at the same time created about 20 new line product-manager positions at the divisions to provide division presidents with adequate assistance.

Carefully screen job applicants to get superior people. Decentralize this procedure progressively as the reliability of the people increases.

Increasingly move decisions downward. Ask managers to report on positive actions taken in that direction. This is a key factor in strengthening the competence of line managers; clearly, nobody is going to improve the quality of decision making by mindlessly following detailed instructions all day.

Set high standards of training and performance. Under firmly established decentralization, training and performance standards are enforced by the divisional managers without any prodding, but at this transition stage corporate top management may need to exert greater control.

Make sure people's advancement is based on performance, not politics or willingness to conform. This is a natural corollary to setting standards.

Encourage—and measure—the upward flow of ideas. This involves much more than the traditional "suggestion box" rotting away in some remote corridor of the slumbering bureaucracy. For details see Chapter 9, which discusses ways to beat the bureaucracy.

Pick out superior problem solvers emerging in the process of revitalizing the division operation, and mark them for advancement.

Periodically evaluate progress to determine when the operation is ready to be given autonomy.

CUTTING FAT AND BUILDING MUSCLE

Decentralizing an operation invariably involves cutting fat at headquarters and building muscle at the divisions. Just how is that to be done? Here are some tips.

Identify unproductive corporate staff positions and cut them or begin shifting them to the operating divisions as appropriate. Some corporate functions may simply duplicate divisional ones, usually resulting in regular conflict and often decision paralysis; those must be cut in a hurry. Other functions are performed in remote style at headquarters when they should in fact be handled by the divisions themselves; those must be shifted. Under Acme-Cleveland's new chief executive Ames, for example, many corporate computer programmers, accountants, market researchers, and assistant VPs in manufacturing, sales, finance, and research were eliminated, but some of those functions, restructured in a more appropriate way, were restored at the division level—for instance, marketing managers, controllers, and vice presidents for engineering were added to certain divisions.*

Cut the overall corporate staff budget and reallocate the resources to the divisions as appropriate. This is a corollary to the preceding step in that the main expense is people. However, such items as corporate jet planes (thriving under centralization thanks to the proliferation of headquarters "nitpicking" meetings) and overblown central computer systems also present welcome opportunities for cuts.

Cutting staff is usually far easier for the newly hired chief executive than for the long-established CEO, who is in the difficult position of having to fire executives he himself has put in place. Thus Acme-Cleveland's CEO Ames, free of psychological ties to the people affected by his actions, made quick

---

* *Business Week,* December 21, 1981.

and deep cuts, whereas Edward R. Telling, chairman of Sears Roebuck, resorted to a massive early-retirement program to eliminate superfluous staff jobs. Similarly, Ford reduced its staff by only 26 percent over two years, compared with an immediate 60 percent cut in staff at Acme-Cleveland.

Reduce layers of management. David T. Kearns, chief executive of Xerox Corp., is cutting headquarters staff to reduce both the number of people and the number of layers of management. Similarly, Ford is trying to reduce its 12 layers of management (reflected in $4 billion per year in staff costs), striving to approach the seven layers of its Japanese competitor Toyota Corp. Acme-Cleveland's Ames believes that there should be no more than one salaried employee for every three hourly production workers. In cutting staff, he left the decision of exactly which positions to eliminate to corporate department and division heads; this automatically resulted in reduction of layers, as about 65 percent of the cuts affected corporate middle-management jobs.*

This approach to trimming fat is sharply opposed to the typical centralized pattern for dealing with economic trouble. To begin with, as pointed out by John M. Stewart, a director at McKinsey & Co., the fat in the centralized corporation usually originates in the misguided practice of randomly rotating managers among the divisions, in the belief that "the professional manager can manage anything."† New managers, having only a hazy idea of the business they're expected to run, surround themselves with staff to advise them—and each staff member soon builds his own mini-empire, making sure his operation is as obscure and complex as possible so as to justify his existence and, hopefully, meteoric rise to the heights of corporate power. Faced with the need to cut costs, which were driven up by a suicidal management-to-worker ratio, the centralized company will:

1. Lay off workers (thus further increasing its management-to-worker ratio).
2. Cut "discretionary" expenses such as advertising and public relations (with spiraling downward effect on sales and revenues).

* Ibid.
† Ibid.

3. When all that doesn't help (it usually doesn't), order each department across the board to cut, say, 10 percent (again, usually affecting workers more than the management ranks).

It doesn't take brilliance to guess the net result of such mechanical cuts: accelerated deterioration of productivity, due to increased ratio of empire-building and -defending managers to production workers.

Taking the Plunge: Implementing RD

The most important prerequisites for radical decentralization are a firm commitment by the corporate chief and his top team to RD; recognition by corporate top management of people as the company's greatest asset, with a commitment to developing people rather than programs; and corporate top management's full trust in division managers.

There are eight basic steps involved in implementing RD, assuming the three prerequisites are met:

1. Top management's commitment to radical decentralization must be transmitted down the line, with no doubt left as to the decision authority of division managers.

2. The decentralized units within the organization must be clearly defined. The definition may be based on:

Natural product groupings (for example, food products, automobiles, sporting goods).
Geographical market areas.
Logical market groupings (for example, retail vs. wholesale).
Physical facilities (say, "all plants in Europe").

Different companies will find different segmentations most useful, depending on their business and their internal composition.

3. Each decentralized unit develops its own:

Strategy.
Planning.
Product development.
Product pricing.
Production of products or services.

4. The CEO of the parent organization meets with the unit leaders—who are, of course, called presidents—to decide on overall corporate strategies. In particular, the following must be covered:

Working-capital requirements of the unit must be defined.

Capital-investment policy must be established: How much is the unit expected to invest in equipment and the like?

Expected profit margin must be defined.

Capitalization method for facilities and equipment must be decided upon: will facilities be bought, rented, or leased?

Required corporate reports must be outlined.

Danger signals must be established, and a corporate strategy set up for dealing with them. Typical early-warning signals include:

- Sales volume significantly below forecast, with expenses not reflecting lower volume.
- Loss of market share (due to poor pricing, distribution, or product, or other factors).
- Cash-flow problems (slow receivables).
- Exceptionally high employee turnover.
- Too high a proportion of capital-equipment expenditures incurred too soon, indicating likelihood of a major budget overrun.
- Research-and-development expenditures below target, indicating lack of product innovation.

5. After these preliminary tasks are accomplished, the unit is given the signal to go ahead with RD. The decentralized unit must not be tied into a central computer system, a corporate salary and benefits administration program, a corporate purchasing program, or corporate marketing and sales programs, except "institutional advertising" aimed at the investment community and concerned with such matters as corporate earnings growth or general business direction as opposed to product presentations. Furthermore, labor relations should be handled at the division level, except where this is precluded by the national labor contract. Also, if there is a corporate consulting group, it must sell its services in direct competition with outside experts so as to prevent backlog and cranking out of unrequested "recommendations."

Unless these functions are decentralized, divisional managers cannot be held accountable for performance. As Edward W. Freher, vice president of personnel at decentralized Northwest Industries, states: "We have no headquarters staff for such functions as manufacturing or marketing, for example, because we couldn't hold operating chiefs accountable for performance if someone at headquarters was deciding which advertising agency to use."* ·

On the other side of the coin, the decentralized units must keep their books in such a way that the information can easily be integrated into the corporate format.

It is particularly important that the decentralized units not be tied into the cash pool of the corporation. In the typical centralized corporation, cash is sent by customers to the parent company's lockbox; the operating divisions themselves never see any cash but must ask Big Daddy for money whenever they need it. This breeds lack of concern about receivables management, because money becomes a meaningless figure—"play money." Under RD, each unit is responsible for its own operating cash.

6. The goal of the division president is to operate his unit as independently as possible, using the corporate parent as *banker,* to whom presentations are made to secure loans.

7. A corporate policy is in force never to transfer people from one decentralized division to another. The purpose of this policy is to discourage people from viewing division jobs merely as steppingstones to higher corporate pastures. With such a policy, loyalty to the division and enthusiasm for the work tend to be much greater.

8. If a division president doesn't work under this arrangement, he is fired.

This process of radical decentralization has little to do with the widespread pseudo decentralization into "profit centers," which Professors Robert H. Hayes and William J. Abernathy of the Harvard Business School assert has created an emphasis on immediate profit at the expense of long-range planning.†
To secure immediate profit, companies of course tend to go for minimum risk, as in minor product-line modification to exploit recognized consumer trends of the day. RD, by con-

---

*Ibid.
†Mortimer R. Feinberg, "Senseless Shifts in Strategies?" *Restaurant Business,* November 1, 1981, p. 86.

trast, creates an environment for the true entrepreneur, who thrives on winning long-range success in the face of risk and sometimes short-range loss. As Hayes and Abernathy note: "Deferring to a market-driven strategy without paying attention to its limitations is, quite possibly, opting for customer satisfaction and lower risk in the short run at the expense of superior products in the future."*

Finally, consider the advice of *Management Practice* (Fall 1981) to the top management of diversified conglomerates:

- Greater use of spinoffs and disinvestments—partial or whole.
- Radical corporate restructuring into coherent structures around products, technologies, etc.
- New organizational forms giving greater asset-allocation power to the divisions on the firing line.
- Other experiments in power sharing between the center and the peripheries of the corporate giant.
- Revised performance measurement for divisional managers to supplement profit and loss evaluations.
- Wherever possible—*simplify!*

*Ibid.

156

CHAPTER 8

Humanizing the Organization

Humanizing the organization is a worthwhile goal in itself, but it also has tangible benefits that translate into substantial boosts to the bottom line. The humane organization:

- Attracts good people.
- Improves the quality of managers by increasing their self-confidence and motivation.
- Keeps good people.
- Puts the fun back into business.

Now let's look at some specific ways to achieve those benefits.

Inspect turnover and morale. Do employees feel they can grow in the company, or do they feel frustrated and dead-ended? If the latter, you'd better read this chapter (and the next) with a magnifying glass.

Focus on development of people, not merely programs and projects. This was mentioned in passing in Chapter 7, but it bears repeating here. People, not products or programs, are the greatest asset of a company.

Screen job applicants carefully to get superior people, not just superior "backgrounds." You want people who think independently, not conformists.

Trust your people, don't police them. Donald E. Peterson, president of Ford Motor Company, studied Toyota's management and concluded that Japanese executives trust their workers and assume they will work as well as they can. By contrast, U.S. executives add layers of staff to check on line operators because they do not trust their subordinates.* The result: decision paralysis, cost explosion, confrontations, and decline of the business.

Keep in mind that independence and authority are just as important to managers as remuneration. Accept the risk inherent in giving managers the power to carry out their projects and programs. As J. Stanford Smith, retired chief of International Paper Company and executive-in-residence at Cornell University Business School, puts it: "You need clearly spelled-out corporate policies indicating that actual business decisions are to be made by line managers, and that no one will second-guess them."†

Reward loyalty. This may seem difficult at times, especially if a long-time employee's performance has begun to slip significantly. Keep in mind that not only is it the decent thing to do, but there are definite payoffs: public reputation as a responsible, humane employer (which helps attract many good people in years to come) and reciprocal loyalty of employees to the company.

Do not lay off employees as soon as there are economic problems. Developing a superior workforce takes a lot of time and patient work; you don't throw it to the winds at the first sign of trouble. Sony and Delta are but two examples of a growing number of companies that realize the value of this philosophy and enjoy its tremendous benefits in loyalty and attraction of top-notch employees.

Have a flexible, personalized system for responding to personnel problems. Is it acceptable in your company for a clerical employee to complain directly to the president about a problem with his paycheck? It is at Delta, and at other enlightened companies. At the least there should be a well-established grievance procedure that enables employees to clear conflicts with their superiors at a higher level.

Don't play chess with people. Some companies still move their managers all over the globe without consulting them, but the number of managers (and families) who accept that kind of

*Business Week, December 21, 1981.
†Ibid.

treatment is shrinking rapidly. Of course, moving people across divisions is definitely out, as discussed in the preceding chapter.

Make sure that those who have to live with a decision have a say in it. At Delta, stewardesses choose their own uniforms. In some companies, mechanics choose their own supervisors. What is gained by this? Motivation, first of all, and a sense of self-worth. And, more often than not, better decisions as well.

Encourage superior performers to redesign their jobs as they see fit. This is related to giving people a say, but goes somewhat further. It is, in fact, one of the cardinal principles of radical decentralization: pushing decisions as far down the line as possible, both to improve the quality of decisions and to develop people.

Stress work goals, not time goals. If people are treated like grade schoolers, they'll act like grade schoolers; if you treat them like responsible people, they'll act accordingly. Time and again, employers have found that productivity rises and falls with motivation, not with rigidly enforced work periods.

Do not base any decisions on numbers or computer printouts alone without proper attention to human factors. I know of one New York miniconglomerate that holds regular "Beat the Computer" rap sessions to correct computer-based decisions and proposals if they conflict with human needs and feelings. However it is done, make sure to steer clear of management by the numbers—it doesn't work.

Encourage managers to rely as much as possible on informal oral communication. This will make business more personal and will speed up decisions. Some companies go as far as declaring a virtual ban on the memo, the favorite tool of the bureaucrat.

If feasible, give retired employees an option to continue working part time, as long as they wish, in appropriate positions. Your experienced retirees are a valuable source of talent, developed with great effort and cost; it seems a foolish practice indeed to let that talent go to waste, as a growing number of companies have come to realize.

Encourage people to stand up for their point of view before superiors. If you stress conformism, you can't expect fresh ideas—they come only from committed people who think for themselves.

Think small. From a certain point of magnitude on, money

159

and operations become unreal, leading to a dehumanized mass-think environment. At Hewlett-Packard, for example, managers are assigned segments no greater than $40 million to $250 million in sales for this reason.*

Bring in customers to meet your employees. Bringing customers and key people together, I have learned, is an excellent way to enhance customer relations while letting your people know they're important and you care about them. At Steelcraft we periodically conducted meetings attended by shipping-department people, customer-relations people, estimators, engineers, production people, and so on, where they had a chance to meet, shake hands with, and interact with customers we sometimes brought in by the busload. One advantage of these meetings was to establish a personal relationship between our key people and customers. Another was to give our technical and production employees unique insights into the customer's use of our products. A third was to give customers a chance to air problems and gripes, and to create an atmosphere in which solutions, and in some cases amicable compromises, could be reached through a joint team effort.

Arrange customer-plant visits. Applying the same psychology, and for the same reasons, we sent foremen, supervisors, engineers, and other technical people to the plants of key customers. There they got a chance to meet and become friendly with customer operations personnel, and at the same time got a break from the day-to-day routine, while their egos were being massaged. In my experience, nothing can quite compare with observing the customer using your product. You see firsthand the problems he runs into from time to time, you see *how* he is using the product, and, if you are knowledgeable, you observe misuse as well as proper use. Once an employee becomes sensitive to the customer's needs, his whole approach to his job tends to change. On top of that, he feels a *personal* responsibility to produce trouble-free products and service, because he has met and now knows the people at the other end of the line.

Brainstorm problems. I don't know how many times I've seen managers mind-boggled by problems they're unable to solve, or unable to solve easily by themselves. Sometimes I wonder

* *The Los Angeles Times,* June 6, 1980.

if they think they're going to get a special award or recognition for coming up with a solution without help. What I've learned in business is that the heroes aren't the lone problem solvers necessarily, but the managers who find the best solution in the shortest possible time. That's one good reason for getting as many of your people as possible into the problem-solving act. Another good reason is that when you ask an employee for help in solving a problem, exercising a judgment, or making a decision, it makes him feel ten feet, six inches tall. It lets him know you respect him as an individual and professional. It makes him feel good and important, and gives his self-confidence a boost. At Steelcraft we conducted frequent ad hoc problem-solving meetings with these objectives in mind—and got better solutions as a side benefit.

Solicit ideas. Most executives in large corporations believe they go to their employees for ideas on how to improve products and service. More often than not they base this belief on the fact that a suggestion box has been set up in the employee cafeteria or elsewhere in the plant. I have no quarrel with suggestion systems. They're certainly better than no system at all. But from what I have seen, you can go a giant step further in encouraging and soliciting employee ideas. How? Simply by asking them. By challenging them. By giving their imagination a prod. At Steelcraft we did this naturally and automatically time and again. I don't know how often, in pre-acquisition days, I would walk over to an employee's desk and ask his opinion about a project or program in the works. "Jim, how do you think we should do this?" "Mary, do you think we could design this brochure more effectively?" "Harry, I'm not happy with the way this door opens and closes; can you come up with any ideas to improve it?"

It doesn't have to be formal. It doesn't have to be a system or program. It doesn't even have to be organized or planned. But it does have to become a way of business life, a way of working with your people, a way of demonstrating your faith in their ability and your respect for their thoughts and ideas.

I sometimes like to project where people are concerned. For example, I like to look beyond the 9:00 to 5:00 work day when Bill goes home to his wife and she says, "Hello, darling, what kind of day did you have?" Most days will necessarily be fairly routine, because that is the nature of events in business and life. But if, every so often, instead of the standard ho-hum reply I can be responsible for having Bill report enthusiastically to his wife, "Guess what, dear? The boss came into my office today, sat down at my desk, and asked what I thought about the new watchamacallit the company has on the drawing boards. Well, here's what I told him. . . ."

It makes a man feel like someone in front of his wife and, more important, it makes him feel like someone deep down within himself.

CHAPTER 9

Breaking Up the Bureaucracy

Bureaucracy is a way to *slot* people and situations—usually by means of "standard operating procedures"—so workers don't have to think or listen. To break up bureaucracy, people must first of all be encouraged to think for themselves and to listen to others. Those two main themes underlie all the advice offered in this chapter.

To evaluate the degree of bureaucratization present in the organization, review the questions listed under "Evaluating the Status Quo" in Chapter 7. Those questions are concerned with such things as:

Action mobility.
Levels of approval.
Risk-taking frequency.
Decisions bogging down in committees.
Managerial meddling.
Entrepreneurial climate.
Authority for planning.
New venture financing.
Employee morale at all levels.
Role of politics in career decisions.
Compensation levels.

Here, are some specific suggestions for dealing with the insidious, ever-ready monster of bureaucracy.

Cut layers of approval for decisions. One of the things to be eliminated is lengthy "justification reports" (usually with several revisions for each of the different editions for the many layers of the management layer cake) for every major expenditure. Such bureaucratic reports are compiled at great cost to the organization:

- Extra paperwork.
- Extra management personnel ("nitpickers") to handle the paperwork load.
- Delays in urgently needed capital acquisitions.
- Forgone months of increased productivity.
- Irrevocably lost opportunities because the competition moved faster.
- Problems needlessly escalated, often to a crisis point.

Encourage risk taking. In the bureaucracy, risky proposals are "weeded out" by computer analysis, whether or not experience and managerial judgment argue for going ahead. It's the nature of risk management that things sometimes don't work out as hoped. What counts is the batting average over the long run—something the centralized "profit center" manager with his eyes glued to the short-term bottom line cannot comprehend.

Have simple, reliable channels for moving "unusual" ideas up the line. If you don't have room for the unusual, you don't have room for innovation. Unusual ideas almost by definition run counter to "standard operating procedures." In the bureaucracy, they would therefore be automatically squelched as heresies against the cherished SOP Bible. Brainstorming sessions, active suggestion systems, and direct access to top division managers by all employees are some obvious ways to keep the channels open and busy.

Keep track of the number of suggestions for change made from the line up. This will give you an idea of the degree of bureaucratization still present and the caliber of the people in the organization.

Keep policies and procedures, and their enforcement, simple and flexible. No policy or procedure can foresee every eventuality, every customer reaction, every move of the competition or the market, so how could it possibly be sacrosanct? And if it takes a team of lawyers to make sense of a policy statement, don't expect your employees to pay any attention to it.

Continuously examine policies, procedures, and organizational structures. Do they serve to keep decision making fast and flexible? That's what policies, procedures, and organizational structures are supposed to do. Unfortunately, they usually accomplish just the opposite—especially if they've been around for a long time without ever being dusted off and adapted to the current business situation.

Control the information explosion. Make sure that the right kind and amount of information is generated so that each manager can do his job properly. Sometimes managers lack crucial information; more commonly, though, they are swamped with irrelevant reports, printouts, memos, and the like.

Make sure that employees are advanced on the basis of their level of performance and record of improvement, not on the basis of company politics or willingness to conform. Rewarding the yes-sayers in one of the surest ways to build a rock-solid bureaucracy.

Make it clear that it is no offense to go over a supervisor's head with suggestions, questions, or complaints. At the least, there must be a formal grievance procedure, but the broader the approach, the better. Remember, you need people who stand up for their ideas and opinions—they may just have that one idea, rejected by their supervisor, that will make millions for the company.

Encourage oral rather than written communication within the company. The bureaucrat prefers the written word because it is impersonal and because he doesn't trust people. If you've got it in a memo, you can "document" your case against the other guy when things go wrong. Encouraging people to trust others may lead them to discover that others are in fact by and large trustworthy—and that's the first step in building that all-important team spirit.

Discourage committees and task forces that are set up to avoid decisions or obfuscate responsibility. If there is one person who should ordinarily make the decision, let that person make it.

Regularly review programs to identify those that no longer are, or never were, beneficial. If you wait too long to remove the deadwood, you may find yourself caught in an all but impenetrable jungle. Just because a program was there yesterday doesn't mean it has to be there tomorrow.

Stress work goals rather than time goals. It's been shown time and again that productivity goes up when people's motivation improves. Make people accountable for *results,* and give them the authority to make the decisions required to perform the job properly.

Identify the major time-wasting activities and take action to eliminate them. The most popular ones include unnecessary meetings, memos with all-encompassing distribution lists, studies and surveys, extended lunch hours under the guise of "informal meetings," and travel to and from meetings.

Resist all efforts to centralize the computer system and the information flow. I needn't repeat here why a central computer system doesn't work. Just remember Levinson's Law of Information Explosion: Paperwork expands to exceed the capacity of the computers installed to create it. What you'll get are backlogs, proliferation of useless and often misguiding reports, and data processing costs that go through the roof.

Watch out for empire building. A sure sign of this is the sprouting of new staff positions, created ostensibly to "advise," but really to dilute decision-making authority and second-guess line managers with standardized "scientific" analyses. Empire building is a natural human tendency, and no organization, however enlightened, is safe from it. In most cases, it isn't corrected until an economic crisis arises. Why not be the exception?

Bring employees and customers together. This was discussed in some detail in the preceding chapter. Employee-customer contact builds employees' sense of personal responsibility, introduces a much needed personal element into the work, sparks new ideas, and generally makes employees more sensitive to customers' needs. All this is a vast improvement over an operation where the view of the customer is clouded by a mass of unbending standard operating procedures.

Control the size of the organization. As Levinson's Law of the Concrete Jungle states: Inefficiency multiplies in direct proportion to the size of the organization.

CHAPTER 10

Being an
Entrepreneurial Leader

One problem that breeds bureaucracy and its debilitating by-products is that many robotized and superregulated managers don't think of their organization as a bureaucracy or of themselves as bureaucrats. I refer to this as the "Who, me?" syndrome. For all practical purposes, I view bureaucracy as an antonym of leadership. If you are an executive employed by a large corporation, how do you see yourself: as a leader or a bureaucrat? Using as much candor and objectivity as you can muster, take the following quiz. It may help you confirm the faith you have in yourself, or reveal a smirch or two on your leadership image that you weren't aware of.

1. If you disagreed with your boss, would you stand up for your viewpoint and defend it, or back down in a hurry?
2. Do you make many suggestions for change, occasional suggestions, or few if any suggestions?
3. In your organization, is *who* you know and support more important than *what* you know?
4. Do you usually have to go through circuitous channels to get information, initiate a procedural change, or get something out of the ordinary approved?
5. Are rules and regulations too "chicken" in your organization to your way of thinking, and too rigidly enforced?
6. Would you characterize your group as fast-moving and flexible, or stodgy and lumbering?

7. Are committees and task forces in evidence all over the place most of the time? Do they usually take too long to decide?
8. Do branch and division managers have very little real authority?
9. Do you get the impression policies and procedures are standardized to the hilt?
10. Does your organization have a relatively high turnover of talented and outstanding key people?
11. Would you say that a person's advancement is generally based on his level of performance and record of improvement?
12. Do you think too many decisions are based on computer printouts, with too little attention paid to human inputs?
13. Does your company employ more than 100 people at corporate headquarters, more than 200, more than 400, more than that?
14. How large a role do you yourself have in setting the performance goals you are expected to meet?
15. Do you feel your company generates enough information for you to do your job properly, too little information, or too much information? Do you often feel swamped by paperwork?

If your answers were open-minded and frank, they should give you some insight into the degree of bureaucracy you are involved in and exposed to, and into whether your response is weak-kneed or courageous. Let's review the questions one at a time:

1. The bureaucrat usually backs down in a hurry.
2. The deep-dyed bureaucrat settles for the status quo.
3. Politics is the bureaucratic name of the game.
4. Almost invariably, the more circuitous the channels, the more deadening the bureaucracy.
5. No organization—or society—could run without rules. But as Robert Burton once wrote, no rule is so general that it admits of no exception.
6. Well-managed companies *spring* into action; bureaucracies crawl.

7. The committee is the bureaucrat's leaning post.
8. Big Daddy, the King of the Bureaucrats, dispenses authority with the miserliness of a Shylock.
9. Mindless standardization is the hallmark of bureaucracy.
10. The smart and insightful key manager views the bureaucratic environment as a stifling and frustrating career pit.
11. Superior performance or not, the only way out of a bureaucratic career rut is too often political.
12. Overdependence on computers breeds and feeds the bureaucracy.
13. It usually follows that the more bodies at headquarters, the more pervasive the bureaucracy.
14. The nonbureaucratic manager usually has a hand in setting his own goals and, as a result, believes in them.
15. The next time you pass by a bureaucrat, if he doesn't see you coming, it's probably because you're hidden by a mountain of paperwork on his desk.

The final question is one you alone can answer. Are you a bureaucrat? Are you employed in a bureaucracy? If so, what are you going to do about it?

Motivating People

Perhaps the greatest difference between the bureaucrat and the true leader is this: The bureaucrat *controls* people by means of standard operating procedures; the leader *motivates and develops* people. The reason the bureaucrat controls people is that he mistrusts them; the reason he doesn't develop them is that he fears losing his position. By contrast, the leader operates on the basis of trust and the self-confidence born from real achievement.

What does it take to motivate people to do a good job? Here are some of the basics.

Show complete confidence in your subordinates. Don't act like a policeman breathing down their necks. Be a member of a team.

Give subordinates real responsibility. This involves risk, but experience shows that it is a risk worth taking. Remember, too, that mistakes are there to be learned from—they're the price you pay for developing superior people who will make the organization soar. What's more, many of the worst "failures" turn out to be the source of highly successful new ideas.

Success breeds success. Support your people; help them experience successes. And reinforce those successes with recognition and congratulation. In helping subordinates, though, remember that there is a fine line between helping and meddling. The meddler leaps into the fray with instructions thinly disguised as "suggestions"—all with the best intentions, of course. The helpful manager asks whether he can be of help or, better yet, waits until he is approached.

As employees experience success in one area, they'll gain confidence that they can perform in other areas as well.

Show subordinates that their opinion matters. Solicit their ideas. Make them feel that they're important members of a team.

Set mutually agreed-upon objectives for your subordinates. To do their jobs well, people must know what is expected of them, and they must have agreed to it. Performance standards must be high, but keep them realistic—you want to stretch people, not tear them in half.

Encourage superior performers to make changes in their jobs. They usually know best what needs to be done and how to do it, so let them. The results will almost always be better, and their sense of self-worth will emerge vastly improved.

Living the Concept of RD

Commit yourself to RD, and transmit that commitment down the line.

Decentralize hiring and training within your domain of responsibility as far as possible. How quickly you achieve this will depend on the caliber of the people already in place.

Have an active suggestion system. Keep asking—and keep listening. Mingle with the troops. Use brainstorming sessions. None of this has to be formal, but if you want the operation to thrive, it must be done.

Don't try to "minimize risk" by basing decisions primarily on computer-generated numbers rather than on your experience and intuition. Remember, the computer is a tool, not a substitute for human judgment. As Robert H. Hayes and William J. Abernathy of the Harvard Business School put it:

The argument that no new product ought to be introduced without managers undertaking a market analysis is common sense. But the argument that consumer analyses and formal market surveys should dominate product development is untenable. It may be useful to remember that the initial market estimate for computers in 1945 projected total worldwide sales of only ten units. Customers may know what their needs are, but they often define those needs in terms of existing products, processes, markets, and prices.*

Help subordinates get sensitive to customers' needs. The best way to do this, as discussed in detail in Chapter 8, is to bring customers and employees into direct contact.

Think for yourself—don't let standard operating procedures do it for you. More on this in Chapter 9.

Evaluate subordinates on the basis of their performance and record of improvement, not on the basis of how well they conform to your views. Surround yourself with independent thinkers, not yes-sayers. It may be less comfortable to live with conflict, but the superior manager not only can put up with that discomfort but actually thrives on it. Who said that life is supposed to be comfortable, anyhow?

Don't shirk responsibility for decisions by delegating them to committees or task forces. By the same token, don't let your subordinates get away with anything. Keep them pointed in the right direction: toward action and responsibility.

Involve subordinates in problem solving and decision making. And watch for outstanding problem solvers and prime them for leadership roles.

Review departmental (divisional, or other) needs regularly and earmark specific employees for training and development with those needs in mind. The objective here is to match individual career goals and qualifications with opportunities for advancement.

Rely on informal personal contact rather than on memos and other written communications. You're the one who sets the tone. If you communicate like a bureaucrat, so will your subordinates. The spoken medium makes business more personal and cuts down on the paper explosion. It also avoids decision delays,

---

* "Managing Our Way to Economic Decline," *Harvard Business Review*, July–August 1980.

thus speeding up problem solving and helping people take advantage of opportunities before the competition moves. Finally, it helps build a spirit of trust and teamwork: not using memos to document all your instructions and actions shows that you feel secure and trust the people you're working with.

To which I would add only one suggestion: *Enjoy it or get out of business!* Because if this way of managing people doesn't give you any pleasure, none ever will.

PART IV

Wave of the Future

CHAPTER 11

The Creatures Are Stirring

It's good to be on the bandwagon, and I can tell you I have plenty of company; in fact, thoughtful managers and students of management are hastily scrambling for space.

Part of the big scramble is evidenced by the industrial-relations revolution that is currently in force. Increasing numbers of top and middle managers are getting the message that business success and sustained profit performance hinge more on the way *people problems* are solved than on the way numbers are juggled in a computer to make tomorrow's bottom line more impressive, and that techniques of motivating humans must be achieved before you can cash in on innovative technology.

Nor are the bandwagon hoppers all profit-squeezed small entrepreneurs. The bigs from GM and GE to P&G and AT&T appear to be equally concerned. It's no accident that one of the hottest trends in business today is toward worker involvement in shop-floor decisions, and quality-of-work-life programs designed to boost product excellence and worker productivity by increasing job satisfaction of employees right down the line. States Michael Sonduck, corporate manager of work improvement at giant Digital Equipment Corp., "One of the most dehumanizing assumptions ever made is that workers work and managers think. When we give shop-floor workers control over their work, they are enormously thoughtful."

Isn't it strange that the Japanese learned and applied this

premise decades ago to their everlasting advantage, as Detroit and others could testify, and it has taken so long for the message to reach this side of the Pacific? And does it require any great stroke of brilliance to appreciate that if a shop worker is dehumanized when treated as a mindless entity, a *manager*, paid presumably to think, must be triply dehumanized?

In the Japanese plant and office, unlike in the majority of U.S. counterpart facilities, the employee, whatever his rank, is dedicated and loyal to the organization, usually for the length of his life; the employee is respected and in turn respects those he works with and works for; the employee is consulted regularly, his opinions and suggestions sought about his work and job, its decisions and problems; the employee is regarded by management as a genuine part of the family, his welfare and well-being as a moral responsibility; he isn't pressured and harassed; if the order flow falters, he isn't laid off. And therein lies the difference between productivity and worker slowdown, between top-quality merchandise and automobile doors with Coke bottles rattling inside them.

But now at last the signs are clear, I believe, that the creatures are stirring. And when they stir, they stir hard. Hopefully, the battle cry from managers and managed alike will soon ring from the "ramparts" of offices, warehouses, and plants throughout the United States: "Watch out, Japan, here we come!"

End of an Era

It is my prediction that the day of the numerologist is slowly drawing to a close. Crippling remote-control management of the kind I described in earlier chapters—in effect, proxy management—is falling into disrepute, not because of humane and humanitarian reasons, but because it is economically and competitively disadvantageous to cling to the demeaning numbers-centered management of the 1960s and 1970s. On top of that, at least so far as the vast majority of line employees is concerned, powerful unions will no longer stand for it.

Smart, observant chief executives won't stand for it either. Increasing numbers of large corporations are "slimming down," spinning off divisions they can't manage comfortably or profitably in what Wall Streeter Stefan D. Abrams calls "enterprise restructuring."

One chief executive I know, who prefers not to be named, refers to his company's tentative plan of enterprise restructuring by a different label: autonomy qualification, meaning that if a division demonstrates the planning and leadership capabilities needed for success, it will be granted autonomy, as opposed to the centralized style of management long practiced. Among his reasons for making the change are complaints from customers and distributors that under the centralized system the company was "unresponsive to local needs."

Author Alvin Toffler sees a sharp swing away from the "Great Centralizers" so long in vogue. "Decentralization," he writes, "has become a hot political issue from California to Kiev."

If "the creatures are stirring," as I believe, much of the unrest is being triggered by centralized discontent. Toffler views the new shift as responsible, at least in part, for the great tax revolt of the late 1970s. "More important," he adds, " 'decentralization' has also become a buzzword in management, and large companies are racing to break their departments into smaller, more autonomous 'profit centers,' " and "most important, we are also radically decentralizing the economy as a whole."* He sees clear signs of a gigantic shift of information flows in America and believes a fundamental decentralization of communications is under way. He cites a recent General Motors meeting where 280 top executives spent two days trying to pinpoint ways to break up bureaucratic patterns and get more decisions made on the firing line. Toffler adds: "It is not possible for a society to decentralize economic activity, communications, and many other crucial processes without also, sooner or later, being compelled to decentralize government decision-making as well."† Norman Macrae, deputy editor of *The Economist,* stated recently that large organizations will have to restructure into "confederations of enterprise."

In my opinion, whether this takes place sooner or later will have a profound and long-lasting effect on the economy.

---

* *The Third Wave,* New York: Morrow, 1980, p. 274.
† Ibid., p. 450.

At the Forefront

Here, as with every new movement, when the sweet scent of a competitive edge is sniffed by profit-hungry chief executives, any number of corporate bandwagon hoppers cautiously starting to decentralize could be cited, and some of them already have been. But almost invariably, at the forefront of the movement is a handful of companies whose chiefs, having read the signs long ago, are far ahead of the rest of the field in applying and cashing in on the management philosophy and human technology involved.

Eagle-Picher Industries, Inc. Eagle-Picher, with sales of about $600 million per year, produces chemicals, machinery, and transportation products in its 24 divisions. The 134-year-old Cincinnati-based company, an unconglomerated conglomerate, has been characterized by *Forbes* as "one of the nation's least-known success stories." Indeed, its profit performance over the past decade or so has been something more than impressive.

The reason? "Decentralization is a virtual religion with us," a vice president acknowledges. The avowal is backed by mountains of evidence. Many large companies have more people employed in the accounting or data processing departments alone than Eagle-Picher has in its corporate headquarters (55). The parent furnishes the capital, but budgets, profits, expansion, new markets, and the like are the division head's responsibility.

The conglomerate's acquisition strategy is to buy small companies—under 500 people—in rural locations, well-managed enterprises with good community ties, and then give them the final word so far as decision making is concerned. States *Forbes:* "Division managers have ultimate responsibility for the direction and product development—sometimes overruling opposing views from corporate headquarters—and are judged on results."*

"Centralization has a robotizing effect on the people," the vice president believes. "People feel freer and function more imaginatively and skillfully when permitted to operate independently."

Independent operation at Eagle-Picher eliminates headquarters meetings that division executives are forced to attend.

*Forbes, August 15, 1977.

178

There is no fixed and rigid corporate planning department or policy. Capital expenditures are discussed and agreed upon in informal conversations, usually over the telephone, between division managers and group vice presidents. There is no centralized corporate computer; computers have a way of producing truckloads of paper, and reports in this company are kept to a minimum.

Salaries are determined for each division by local management according to market need and demand. Fifty-nine different pension plans are in force, again on a customized need basis, with no standardization attempted.

Many centralized, brainwashed corporate "experts" would be highly critical of Eagle-Picher's "loose" administration and management, and could probably come up with all kinds of arguments to prove why it isn't efficient. But on one point they would be in no position to argue—the organization's performance track record, the loyalty and high morale at the divisions.

I asked the vice president, "If you operate so successfully this way, why do so few corporations follow suit?"

He has his own theory in response to this question: "For radical decentralization to work, you need very secure people at the top of the company. Otherwise, the system could be threatening."

Beatrice Foods Co. What happens when a radically decentralized corporation runs into deep problems at corporate headquarters? Nothing much, at least so far as its divisions are concerned. To wit, when Chicago-based Beatrice Foods' top brass locked horns in a skirmish for control toward the end of the 1970s—a contest that has been known to shake and break the hardiest centralized company—it was barely noticed in the field. As business writers Stanley H. Brown and Marcia Berss stated the case, the sprawling decentralized enterprise continued to thrive almost without regard to what was going on at headquarters.*

Echoed a *Barron's* report: "Outsiders who voiced alarm at recent brawling within top management and problems with acquired companies couldn't have reckoned with the fact that the financial record would remain unblemished through all the

Forbes, April 30, 1979.

troubles. But it has, much to the credit of the company's diverse interests and decentralized operating style." *

Needless to say, it takes more than diverse interests and decentralized style to produce and perpetuate profit performance, and if an industry turns sour or a product line trips over a competitor's brilliant innovation, it will take more than autonomy to bring customers back to the fold. But if a business is healthy and a management team strong, radical decentralization will help ensure that they remain robust, and Beatrice Foods, with sales exceeding $3 billion annually, looked upon by some analysts as the *Wunderkind* of the industry, has certainly made the most of this reality.

Referring back to the seven keys described in Chapter 7, Beatrice has each one of them carved out of the toughest tool steel. Under the 24-year generalship of William G. Karnes, the company has consistently managed to master the delicate technique of granting unit-and-management-building autonomy on the one hand throughout its wide-ranging empire and, on the other, providing the financial support and control that motivated the acquisitions to begin with.

Curtice-Burns, Inc. If any corporation has profit-center management "down to a science" it is Beatrice Foods, so it is no wonder the company has its imitators and emulators, although Rochester New York's, Curtice-Burns, Inc., a growing food conglomerate with 17 years of decentralized experience behind it, can't fairly be classified a copy cat.

Curtice-Burns, whose sales climbed to approximately $300 million in less than two decades and whose earnings per share rocketed almost 600 percent in a recent ten-year period, has a headquarters staff of only 12. I can recall a corporate personnel manager in one centralized conglomerate who had 12 people reporting to him. Here each division has a chief executive officer, according to president and CEO Hugh Cumming. "He is completely responsible for that business, other than major capital investments."

To what does Cumming attribute the success of the conglomerate's seven divisions? He doesn't use the label specifically, but it boils down to radical decentralization. Among his precepts and qualifiers:

Barron's, January 14, 1980.

• The company will acquire no business without the assurance of a management team with an outstanding track record, and one that will remain at the helm. It's a tough bill to fill, Cumming concedes, but one that is well worth the effort. The philosophy attracts competent suitors who like to run their own show.

• Each "profit center retains its own regionally famous name (such as Blue Boy in the Northeast, Nalley's out West, Snyder's in Ohio and Pennsylvania) and stands on its own. The corporate logo is inconspicuously placed at the bottom of each product.

• Entrepreneurship is advocated and encouraged. Whether a division chief executive runs an operation that does $10 million or $85 million a year, he runs it as if the business were his own.

• Management is by exception rather than control. Corporate executives stick their noses into the pudding only if it starts to go sour. Admittedly, knowing when to get into the act is the toughest decision to make in a decentralized setup. Too much interference breaks down confidence and morale; waiting too long can be costly. "We, as managers," says Cumming, "have to have failures to learn. If every time you have a failure, you get into the act, nobody's going to take any chances."*

For several years, Cumming told an American Management Associations Forum, "The company has had a policy of maximizing the divisions and streamlining headquarters. "We couldn't accommodate more staff if we wanted to," he quipped, "there's no more room in the building."

Teledyne Inc. For hands-off management at its profit-building best, you could turn to no better model than this Los Angeles amalgam of 130 companies that produce a hodgepodge of products from shower heads to seismic systems that monitor earthquakes. Declares *New York Times* writer N. R. Kleinfield, "To a large extent, Teledyne is the creation of one man. The man is Henry Singleton, an unorthodox and remarkable businessman who is high on almost everybody's list of the ten most effective executives in the country."

*"Food Conglomerate Gives Autonomy, Gets Results," *Management Review,* November 1979.

181

Little wonder. Teledyne prospered during the go–go years of the 1960s when conglomerates came into their own, prospered during the Great Disenchantment of the 1970s when most conglomerates fell from a hundred–plus dollars per share to $10 or less, and continues to prosper today. Despite scores of wholly owned divisions and substantial holdings in such companies as Curtiss-Wright (57 percent), Brockway Glass (29 percent), Litton Industries (25 percent), and lesser holdings in H. J. Heinz, International Harvester, Walter Kidde, and others, Singleton has no interest in meddling in the management of companies which he controls or in which he has clout. If they want me, he says, I'm as close as the telephone. He gets very few calls.

Kleinfield describes Teledyne as "relatively decentralized." I've heard one astute analyst interpret this assessment as "decentralized wherever the size, quality of management, and independence of the operation allow." Singleton promotes and encourages autonomy as a prime profits motivator. The *Times* man tells of one division, Teledyne Systems, which had a department that produced hybrid electronic circuits for in-house consumption. When the department began to sell to outside customers and succeed at it, Singleton created a separate company called Teledyne Microelectronics.

So far as size is concerned, the CEO equates too large with unwieldy. Notes Kleinfield: "As distinct from the fashion of many conglomerates of merging companies in related businesses together, Teledyne fastidiously believes in keeping things small. What better way, it figures, to motivate company managers and to smoke out ills before they turn cancerous."*

These are but three of the brightest shining stars in decentralized orbit today. I suspect that a year or two from now, many large powerful conglomerates, having assessed the ills of remote-control management and layerism, will be riding the bandwagon as well. I have no doubt that at this point scores of astute chief executives in medium–size and big corporations must be studying the feasibility of radical decentralization and weighing the benefits.

Indeed, many "restructured enterprises" in a diversity of U.S. industries are currently in various phases of reorganiza-

---

* *The New York Times,* February 1, 1981.

tion. In 1977, for example, then-chairman Frederick J. Port of ESB Ray-O-Vac Corp. decided that what the company needed to make better use of its product and technological savvy was closer ties between corporate headquarters and its operating divisions. So he installed a layer of four executive vice presidents, each responsible for an assortment of products, corporate functions, and geographical areas.

Living with the system was tougher than implementing it, recalls a former senior vice president, who describes the decision-making process as "very cluttered." It was uncluttered by David C. Dawson, who, on Port's death, took the reins. He delayered the organization and did away with corporate supervision, which he felt had a stifling effect. His reorganization called for wholesale decentralization.*

Philips, the Dutch electronics giant, has been having its problems in recent periods, with after-tax profits falling in half. In most operations throughout Europe, the organization is highly centralized and strongly controlled from its Eindhoven headquarters. Certainly much of its trouble stems from its great lumbering movement, at least one close observer believes. He cites the organization's slow-moving pace in such areas as mainframe computers, random-access memory chips, word processing systems, and personal computers, to name some specifics. "The corporate hound can lift its head by itself," he quips, "but it needs assistance in raising its rump."

An exception to the corporate norm appears to be Philips' American arm, North American Philips Corp., where, according to vice chairman Frank L. Randall, Jr., autonomy reigns. He avows to a *Business Week* reporter that the arrangement between NAP and Philips is no more than "a very close, buy-and-sell relationship. . . . There are no coordinating meetings to formulate joint marketing strategies. In contrast to its parent, states an analyst, NAP is "fast-moving and aggressive." The reason, says Randall, is the U.S. company's "complete independence." "We feel we can be of better service to Philips shareholders this way," he adds.†

Another example is Esmark, Inc., a Chicago-based behemoth in a variety of operations from food and fertilizers to

---

* Business Week, March 12, 1979.
† Business Week, March 30, 1981.

women's foundation garments and insurance. When chairman Robert Reneker agreed with critics that the organization was growing unwieldy and cumbersome, he decided to restructure it into "bite-size profit centers," approximately 1,000 of them, each responsible for its own bottom line. Decision making thus has been effectively shifted from headquarters to the boondocks, wherever they may be. Dozens of adjustments and reshufflings have been made since the original move, and are still being made. But control of virtually all aspects of management but capital expenditure has been essentially decentralized in line with the growing national trend.

Or, more precisely, *international* trend, and not only on the corporate scene. Political decentralist movements have taken form and are growing in Western Europe and elsewhere in the world. An outstanding example is France. Notes author Frederick Painton in an article describing President François Mitterand's election victory in May 1981:

> One of his [Mitterand's] instincts has convinced him of the need to decentralize the French government. Borrowing an idea from fellow Socialist Michel Rocard, he proposes to replace the Paris-appointed prefects who preside over the nation's 95 *départements* with locally elected officials. The aim: to put government back in the hands of the people. Mitterand will also push for greater worker participation in the management of companies.*

Whether he can do it without socializing the life out of industry remains to be seen.

Whatever the case, one thing seems to be certain: decentralization of business and government is an idea whose time appears to have come.

Leading the Fight Against Bureaucracy

I've been frustrated again and again by the stultifying bureaucracy that is a by-product of centralized management. But not *all* large corporations are hopelessly bogged down by bureaucracy. Not *all* managers are insensitive to the problems triggered by the depersonalization and dehumanization of

---

* *Time,* May 18, 1981.

business. Not *all* managers rely solely on computer printouts. Not *all* chief executives are so preoccupied with today's bottom-line performance that they are oblivious to human problems and needs.

Yes indeed, there are silver linings and, I suspect, a growing number of them as more and more thoughtful executives wonder why so many American corporations are in trouble, why a nation like Japan can capture 23 percent of the U.S. automobile market and make inroads into a host of other markets ranging from steel and textiles to television and office machines. Not only are a growing number pondering the situation, a growing number are doing something about it as well. For example:

Cooper-Bessemer Co. Alert to the importance of personalized management and encouraging employees to voice their ideas, opinions, complaints, and criticism, CB's "Action" program includes distribution of self-sealing letters to the president. The self-sealers are inserted into the monthly company magazine. Letters must be signed, but if a box on the form is checked, it ensures anonymity. This is an idea that seems to be gaining increased acceptance in industry as more and more concerned managers come to realize that for an enterprise to succeed, it must use the computer as a tool, not a dehumanizer. Another company hopping this bandwagon calls its share-your-thoughts-with-the-president program "Write to Know."

Bastian-Blessing Co. Under the dehumanized centrobureaucracy, it all too often becomes mindless routine to treat people as function-related numbers instead of human beings. Thus employees are moved by the number, promoted, terminated, or temporarily laid off by the number, and put out to pasture when their number runs out. Not at BB. Retired workers are kept on part time if they wish, to apply hard-won skills to new jobs. At the company's "Pioneer Shop," retirees perform a variety of tasks on a flexi-hour basis, some continuing to work productively into their eighties.

Texas Instruments. People at TI are humanized and debureaucratized Japanese style. From chairman Mark Shepherd, Jr., to file clerk Sally Jones, employees lunch in the same cafeteria. Individual motivations and feelings are considered in making crucial career decisions. For example, management reasoned, it doesn't make sense to take a dedicated scientist or

185

engineer away from the lab work he loves and promote him into an administrative job as a VP or manager. So an alternative career path of fellows and senior fellows was initiated to match their compensation to that of the administrative job they might have advanced to and, at the same time, provide the recognition and status every human being thrives on. Memos at TI are for the most part *verboten,* informal personal contact used instead.*

New York miniconglomerate. The game here is called "Beat the Computer." Periodic brainstorming sessions are held at which key managers and supervisors are encouraged to speak their minds regarding company programs, projects, and decisions. Special sensitivity is shown to rules or mandates that stem from systems analysis and cold facts gleaned from computer printouts that might be in conflict with human feelings and needs. In one case, for example, a study determined it was "an unprofitable use of expensive supervisory time" for regional sales managers to visit customers periodically, as was the practice. This mandate was rescinded when the word came through from reps in the field that buyers enjoyed and commented favorably on the personal attention they were receiving from top marketing people.

Hewlett-Packard Co. "It's hard to move from an environment where everybody knew one another to one of 55,000 employees," notes executive vice president Dean Morton. But HP tries. In an effort to defeat the bureaucracy, the company keeps key managers "thinking small" by giving them responsibility for segments of the business ranging from $40 million to $250 million in annual sales. It also spurns long-term debt. The objective: to guarantee employees continuity of employment.†

Wisconsin machinery producer. One effective way to combat bureaucracy, this company's chief executive believes, is to counter the conformity big-company management too often generates. Here anticonformity tenets are published by the personnel department and distributed to key managers, and performance is monitored by the president and his closest aides. These are:

The Los Angeles Times, June 6, 1980.
†Ibid.

1. Keep managerial pipelines open at all times to new ideas. If, for whatever reason, an idea is unacceptable, get back to the suggester within two weeks' time, explaining why, thanking him for his effort, and making a favorable note of the effort on his personnel record.

2. Increase delegation and along with it authority and responsibility on an ongoing basis. Managers are required to report specific action along these lines to superiors.

3. Encourage superior performers to do their jobs as they see fit, and to introduce changes where they feel they are merited.

4. Get subordinates involved in problem-solving and decision-making tasks. Spot for outstanding problem solvers and decision makers, and prime these employees for future leadership jobs.

5. Review departmental needs on a regular basis and earmark specific employees for training and development with needs in mind, the objective being to match individual career goals and qualifications to opportunities for advancement.

Sony Corporation. It's no accident that Japanese-style management is running rings around U.S. centralized superbureaucracies in terms of performance and profit. Time clocks are banned from Sony's San Diego plant. Employees confer regularly with high-level executives, are encouraged to discuss work problems and goals, and air complaints and opinions. "Working for Sony," states one production worker, "is like working for your family." Vice president Masayoshi ("Mike") Morimoto has mastered Spanish so that he can converse with his many Hispanic employees. Hot lines have been set up so that workers can register gripes anonymously if they wish. Despite slowdowns and setbacks in the television industry, not a single Sony employee has been laid off since 1972 when the plant was opened.*

What does all this prove in the end? You don't have to be small to sidestep bureaucratization. But you have to *think* small. you have to break down the mass-think environment. In a nutshell, you have to decentralize radically with individual needs and performance in mind.

---

* *Time,* March 30, 1981.

Index

189